Jesus

Jesus

 A Meditation on His Stories
and
His Relationships with Women

ANDREW GREELEY

A Tom Doherty Associates Book
New York

JESUS: A MEDITATION ON HIS STORIES
AND HIS RELATIONSHIPS WITH WOMEN

Copyright © 2007 by Andrew M. Greeley Enterprises, Ltd.

This book is printed on acid-free paper.

A Forge Book
Published by Tom Doherty Associates, LLC
175 Fifth Avenue
New York, NY 10010

www.tor.com

Forge® is a registered trademark of Tom Doherty Associates, LLC.

Library of Congress Cataloging-in-Publication Data

Greeley, Andrew M., 1928–
    Jesus : a meditation on his stories and his relationships with
women / Andrew M. Greeley.—1st ed.
        p.   cm.
    ISBN-13: 978-0-765-31776-6
    ISBN-10: 0-765-31776-1
    1. Jesus Christ—Parables—Meditations. I. Title.

BT375.3 .G74   2007
226.8'06—dc22

                                        2006050936

First Edition: March 2007

Printed in the United States of America

0   9   8   7   6   5   4   3   2   1

For Leo Mahon, who called to my attention the importance of Jesus' use of the kingdom of heaven imagery, and in honored memory of two of my mentors in the study of the Scriptures, Roland Murphy and Raymond Brown. I am also grateful for the comments of John Shea and Timothy Luke Johnson.

In the kingdom, mercy is always a surprise.
ROBERT FUNK

✾

The Parables are . . . the most characteristic
of the speech forms that Jesus employed
and . . . a rich field for investigating . . .
Jesus' Religious Imagination.
SEAN FREYNE

✾

God is nothing but mercy and love.
THERESE

Jesus

❧ INTRODUCTION ❧

WE MUST BEGIN a search for understanding some of
the stories of Jesus with the realization that he is
deliberately elusive, mysterious, enigmatic, paradoxical.
Hence we will never finish our search. We will never understand him. He is a man of surprises, appropriate for one
who claims to witness a God of surprises. Thus, when we
think we at last have figured him out, truly understand
him, and can sign him up for our cause, we find that he has
slipped away. When we are convinced that we can quote
him in support of our own side in any argument, Jesus is
out of here. The Jesus we have shaped to fit our ideas, our
needs, our fears, may be a very interesting and special person, but he's no longer Jesus. We must begin our story of
Jesus by granting him permission to surprise us endlessly—
not that he needs our permission because he will surprise
even without our permission.

Those who followed him in Palestine a couple of millennia ago were fascinated by his stories. They had heard most
of them before, but he insisted on ending the stories with
a disturbing twist, a disconcerting finale. Troubled and

confused, they continued to follow him, if only to see what kind of outrageous paradox or contorted ending he would tell the next time. His good news indeed sounded good, perhaps too good to be true, but it didn't fit the expectations of his followers, even the closest followers. It disturbed them. He disturbed them.

If he doesn't disturb us, then he's not Jesus.*

The disturbance begins at the beginning with the Christmas stories, those preludes to two of the Gospels that charm us today because we are so familiar with them, at the risk of losing strange, almost weird content of the stories.

---

* I call this book a "meditation" because it is a reflection on more than a half century of Sunday preaching and almost that long a time of writing homily notes for priests. Moreover, as a *seanachie*, an Irish storyteller, I am ever more fascinated by the skill in the stories of Jesus and his insidious ability to surprise.

I intend this meditation as a pastoral exercise, not an academic exegetical or theological study. I leave those tasks to those who are more qualified than I am. For the last ten years these homily notes have appeared on my Web page—www.agreeley.com. The time line of Jesus' public life is not my concern in this meditation, nor do I propose a systematic account of his life and death, because others have done these tasks better than I can. Rather I will focus on incidents and stories that are essential to understand how he experienced the Father-in-Heaven, who, if Jesus is to be believed, is even more surprising.

The Christmas Surprises

At that time Emperor Augustus ordered a census to be taken throughout the Roman Empire. When this first census took place, Quirinius was the governor of Syria. Everyone, then, went to register himself, each to his own hometown.

Joseph went from the town of Nazareth in Galilee to the town of Bethlehem in Judea, the birthplace of King David. Joseph went there because he was a descendant of David. He went to register with Mary, who was promised in marriage to him. She was pregnant, and while they were in Bethlehem, the time came for her to have her baby. She gave birth to her first son, wrapped him in cloths and laid him in a manger—there was no room for them to stay in the inn.

There were some shepherds in that part of the country who were spending the night in the fields, taking care of their flocks. An angel of the Lord appeared to them, and the glory of the Lord shone over them. They were terribly afraid, but the angel said to them, "Don't be afraid! I am here with good news for you, which will bring great joy to all the people. This very day in David's town your Savior was born— Christ the Lord! And this is what will prove it to you: you will find a baby wrapped in cloths and lying in a manger."

Suddenly a great army of heaven's angels appeared with the angel, singing praises to God: "Glory to God in the highest heaven, and peace on earth to those with whom he is pleased!"

When the angels went away from them back into heaven, the shepherds said to one another, "Let's go to Bethlehem and see this thing that has happened, which the Lord has told us."

So they hurried off and found Mary and Joseph and saw the baby lying in the manger. When the shepherds saw him, they told them what the angel had said about the child. All who heard it were amazed at what the shepherds said.

Mary remembered all these things and thought deeply about them. The shepherds went back, singing praises to God for all they had heard and seen; it had been just as the angel had told them.

LUKE 1:1–2

TWO LOVELY STORIES, right? One needs only a Christmas tree, carols in the background, and softly falling snow (accumulation one inch or less, please) to create just the right atmosphere of sentimentality. We have perhaps seen so many Christmas cards during our lives that we are immune to the absolute weirdness of the nativity stories— an angel wanders into a hut in Nazareth and tells a very young woman (fifteen perhaps) that she is about to conceive a child of the Holy Spirit. The young woman, who is probably illiterate, asks how this is to be and then recites a complex poem steeped in the language of the Jewish Scriptures and makes the astonishing prediction that all nations will call her blessed. What's going on here?

Then she and her husband (who is not the child's father) go off on a difficult journey in the middle of winter (which is usually quite unpleasant in the mountains of Palestine) and the newborn babe is laid in a pile of straw in a cave somewhere. Then a crew of angels appears in the sky and praises the new babe, whom the shepherds dash over to inspect—shepherds, the absolute bottom of the Jewish social structure, dirty, smelly, rough, ignorant, and religiously unclean men. And what's this about the magicians? Jews were not supposed to believe in magic and certainly not in gentile magic. What's this all about? Is this a decent way for the expected of the nations, the anointed one, the messiah to come into the world? Is this not revisionism of the Prophets and vigorous revisionism at that?

The whole collection of Christmas stories in Matthew's and Luke's Gospels must be called bizarre, surprising indeed but strange, almost offensively so. We don't know where they come from, who wrote them, and how they found their way into the two Gospels.* However, if we understand that the adult Jesus was also surprising, strange, disturbing, and also often more than a little weird, the nativity stories are good "trailers" (as they now call what we used to dub "previews of coming attractions") for the stories yet to come. If we could hear the Christmas stories as though we were hearing them for the first time, we would be shocked or at least awakened out of our usual boredom. This babe who was born in Bethlehem was likely to be one very odd man when he grew up.

Moreover, whoever put the stories together did so with a keen eye on the Jewish Scriptures and made allusions to passages in the Jewish Bible that only someone steeped in those books could have noted. Two questions arise immediately from our contemporary obsessions about literalism. Who wrote these tales and are they true? And a third question might be: why are the stories in Luke and Matthew so different?

In all probability the nativity stories floated, drifted around in the traditions of the followers of Jesus in the middle and late middle of the first century. Someone may have combined them into a catena of stories that was available to St. Luke and he appended them to his Gospel. Unless

---

* Father Raymond Brown in his monumental (731 pages!) book *The Birth of the Messiah* suggests that the canticles in the story originated in a small Jewish Christian group called the *anawin* (Poor People), one of the many diverse groups in the Judaism of that era that was more a religious culture than an organized religion at that time. Perhaps the stories came with the canticles or perhaps Luke obtained the stories elsewhere but inserted the canticles because they seemed appropriate. These songs rely heavily on the Psalms and through the Psalms on Isaiah whose writings had a powerful influence on Jesus.

I am completely mistaken about Luke he was not unaware of the surprises crammed into the stories and how they foretold a lot more surprises from the adult Jesus.

Are they true? There was no video camera ready for the conversation between Mary and Gabriel, nor a stenographer, nor any witness at all. Are those the exact words they exchanged? Who knows? However, given the people involved and the matter at hand, there is a certain verisimilitude in the conversation—at least till we get to the words of the Magnificat, which seem to be unlikely in the mouth of a young peasant woman, but perhaps not impossible. A virginal conception? That of course boggles the mind, though there can be no doubt that was what the author of the story and Luke who collated the story into his Gospel also believed. Such a belief must have existed among some Christians in the late middle years of the first century, so it will not do to claim that it is something that "the Church" imposed in subsequent years. It is of course a scientific impossibility, which is why many Christians reject it today. In a closed universe such conceptions simply do not occur. Yet how closed is the universe?

Father Raymond Brown describes the infancy narratives as theologumenons—stories with a theological point. The author(s) of the narratives were teaching powerful theological truths through their narratives—the most powerful of which is that something utterly new happened with the coming of Jesus, something unexpected, confounding, disorienting, and monumentally surprising: the birth of a new creation or a rebirth of the old (same thing), not only news, but exorbitantly good news. If one can accept that truth then the possibility of a virginal conception—or a resurrection—should seem no big deal. Those who are so eager to reject a virginal conception never seem to pay any attention to the beginning of a new creation, the birth of a second Adam. Either Jesus was what he said he was or he was not. If he was, then there was a special intervention outside the human system (the nature of which we do not understand). If he was not, then his whole story is either fraud or self-deception. Those who would remove from the Jesus story the wondrous, the marvelous, the miraculous, the incredible surprise, destroy the story altogether.

The Christmas stories are either superstitious, if beautiful, nonsense or they tell us something critically important about the babe and about the man he would grow up to be.

The infancy stories of great men of the ancient world are usually spectacular. Signs and portents abound. The Jesus stories, however, are almost drab by comparison. One angel and one maiden, a visit to a cousin who is also miraculously pregnant, a journey to Bethlehem, angels on a hillside, shepherds and magicians, a lost boy in Jerusalem, all rather commonplace. One or two miraculous interventions, but certainly in a low key. Some poetic outbursts that seem a little excessive—how dare this girl child claim that she will be praised by all future generations, a prediction that must have seemed excessive to the collector of the story and perhaps to Luke himself.

She was right, of course. Or whoever put the words in her mouth was right. These thoughts always give me pause. What was going on here, I ask. And I find no answers, save for the thousands of Madonna images that Christian art has produced. Did she really foresee them? Or did the ghost writer?

The power of the infancy narratives is not therefore in their spectacular rhetoric but rather in the astonishing assertions they make in ordinary, commonplace contexts. Surprises in a minor key that rattle the structures of human history, not unlike, come to think of it, the parables themselves. The compilers of the Christmas stories were utterly matter-of-fact about their claims. They did not need to embroider the claims with dramatic events. The substance of the surprise was enough.

But note the surprises that run through the stories— Mary is surprised by the words of the angel. Joseph is surprised by the same angel. Elizabeth is surprised by her elderly pregnancy and by the reaction of her child when Mary comes to visit. The concatenation of surprises leads Mary to the Magnificat. Zachary is surprised by the promise of an heir. His friends and colleagues are surprised by the name given the little boy. The shepherds are surprised by the angels. The Holy Family is surprised by the shepherds' visit and the subsequent appearance of the gentile magicians and the warning to depart into Egypt. Later Mary and Joseph are surprised by Jesus' behavior in the temple. The stories are intoxicated by surprise. To ask whether all these stories must be taken literally is to miss the point completely: surprises rained down on those who were involved—hints powerful enough for them that the greatest surprise in human history had occurred, although almost no one had noticed. The world had been turned upside down, as G. K. Chesterton once remarked, and from this perspective it had suddenly made sense. Or in the words of John Henry Newman, "The Infinite was in swaddling clothes, Omnipotence in bonds." The Word was made flesh and pitched his tent among us. The Kingdom of God was at hand.

Was it really?

It is difficult to understand how someone who denies this surprise can claim to be a follower of Jesus.

Why, however, did the Father-in-Heaven choose this odd style for producing the biggest surprise of all?

To try to understand the Father-in-Heaven is, as a seminary classmate complained to me, an effort at unscrewing the inscrutable. "Where were we?" the Father-in-Heaven might point out as he did to Job when he created the stars.

Fair question, but we can speculate a little from the hints he has left lying around. We began to understand the physical universe when we discovered protons and electrons, the tiny, misty building blocks of all that is. Then we discovered "the singularity," the tiny spot that, when it exploded, produced everything that is, including the biopolymers that would make our human life here on this miserable little planet possible and our minds, working in a relatively small brain, a reflection, as Père Teilhard put it, of the whole evolutionary process. The Father-in-Heaven delights in mystery. In truth, I suspect he revels in it. Why should this vast cosmos, built up with such tiny building blocks, fit the models of advanced mathematics that our frail human intellects in their most playful moods have pasted together? Why should he bother to send Jesus to reassure us that what we fear to hope is, in fact, true—at the center of all creation is the greatest surprise of all, his impassioned and implacable love?

Beats me.

In my more troublemaking moods I contend that God is a comedienne, sometimes even a playful teenage comedienne who enjoys mystery, wonder, and especially surprise—and surprise parties. More seriously I argue that it is God's nature to play, that God has no other choice but to play and love because that is what God is. Not only is playfulness of creation itself a trailer for the Jesus story, not only the playfulness of the Big Bang and the biopolymers, not only the hint that God is impassioned love, so is the playfulness of the Christmas stories. The babe in the manger will die, but that is not the end of the story. The Father-in-Heaven is also and necessarily the God of happy endings, which are the biggest surprise of all. All will be well, all manner of things will be well, as Blessed Juliana promised.

How the Father-in-Heaven will work out all the happy endings is beyond us, but Christmas and the Resurrection and the parables are a promise of happy endings and Christmas is the trailer promising all that will come. The three canticles that should be read as part of a single contribution are the musical background for the Christmas narratives.

THE MAGNIFICAT

Mary said, "My heart praises the Lord; my soul is glad because of God my Savior, for he has remembered me, his lowly servant! From now on all people will call me happy, because of the great things the Mighty God has done for me. His name is holy; from one generation to another he shows mercy to those who honor him. He has stretched out his mighty arm and scattered the proud with all their plans. He has brought down mighty kings from their thrones, and lifted up the lowly. He has filled the hungry with good things, and sent the rich away with empty hands. He has kept the promise he made to our ancestors and has come to the help of his servant Israel. He has remembered to show mercy to Abraham and to all his descendants forever!"

THE BENEDICTUS

"Let us praise the Lord, the God of Israel! He has come to the help of his people and has set them free. He has provided for us a mighty Savior, a descendant of his servant David. He promised through his holy prophets long ago that he would save us from our enemies, from the power of all those who hate us. He said he would show mercy to our ancestors and remember his sacred covenant. With a solemn oath to our ancestor Abraham he promised to rescue us from our enemies and allow us to serve him all the days of our life.

"You, my child, will be called a prophet of the Most High God. You will go ahead of the Lord to prepare his road for him, to tell his people that they will be saved by having their sins forgiven. Our God is merciful and tender. He will cause the bright dawn of salvation to rise on us and to shine from heaven on all

*those who live in the dark shadow of death, to guide
our steps into the path of peace."*

THE NUNC DIMITIS

*"Now, Lord, you have kept your promise, and you
may let your servant go in peace. With my own eyes I
have seen your salvation, which you have prepared in
the presence of all peoples: A light to reveal your will
to the Gentiles and bring glory to your people Israel."*

The canticles we encounter in St. Luke are musical
background for the Christmas narratives, the first Christmas carols, though they are not like any subsequent carols.
If the community of Jewish Christians composed the canticles because they fit the stories that they were telling, it is
not impossible that they were sung during the recitation of
the Christmas narratives.

Mary's *Magnificat* can be read as a celebration by the
"Poor People" of the wonderful deeds God performs for those
who realize their own poverty and weakness and their ultimate dependence on God's love, exactly as they saw the
utter trust in God that marked the Mother of Jesus. They
imposed their theology on Mary and praised her for her
humble acceptance of it. They saw the Christmas surprise
as indeed coming from the Jewish heritage but also as des-
tined for all people who will praise Mary for her courage, a
theme of universalism that will occur often in the Gospel
stories.

In the *Benedictus* Zachary sees the stories of Mary and
Elizabeth, Jesus and John, as evidence of the graciousness

of God, yes to Israel but also to all humankind, in his bright dawn of hope to those who live in the dark shadow of death. Finally Simon at the presentation of Jesus in the temple becomes quite explicit: Jesus is a wonderful surprise, a light to the gentiles and glory to Israel. The theme of Jews bringing the light to the gentiles is clear in some of the books of the Jewish Scriptures, yet remained somewhat scandalous to the Jews of Jesus' time. He would push this surprise to its absolute limit.

A Surprise on the Highway

On that same day two of Jesus' followers were going to a village named Emmaus, about seven miles from Jerusalem, and they were talking to each other about all the things that had happened. As they talked and discussed, Jesus himself drew near and walked along with them; they saw him, but somehow did not recognize him. Jesus said to them, "What are you talking about to each other, as you walk along?"

They stood still, with sad faces. One of them, named Cleopas, asked him, "Are you the only visitor in Jerusalem who doesn't know the things that have been happening there these last few days?"

"What things?" he asked.

"The things that happened to Jesus of Nazareth," they answered. "This man was a prophet and was considered by God and by all the people to be powerful in everything he said and did. Our chief priests and rulers handed him over to be sentenced to death, and he was crucified. And we had hoped that he would be the one who was going to set Israel free! Besides all *that, this is now the third day since it happened. Some of the women of our group surprised us; they went at dawn to the tomb, but could not find his body. They came back saying they had seen a vision of angels who told them that he is alive. Some of our group went to the tomb and found it exactly as the women had said, but they did not see him."*

Then Jesus said to them, "How foolish you are, how slow you are to believe everything the prophets said! Was it not necessary for the Messiah to suffer these things and then to enter his glory?" And Jesus explained to them what was said about himself in all the Scriptures, beginning with the books of Moses and the writings of all the prophets.

As they came near the village to which they were going, Jesus acted as if he were going farther; but they held him back saying, "Stay with us; the day is almost over and it is getting dark." So he went in to stay with them. He sat down to eat with them, took the bread, and said the blessing; then he broke the bread and gave it to them. Then their eyes were opened and they recognized him, but he disappeared from their sight. They said to each other, "Wasn't it like a fire burning in us when he talked to us on the road and explained the Scriptures to us?"

They got up at once and went back to Jerusalem, where they found the eleven disciples gathered together with the others and saying, "The Lord is risen indeed! He has appeared to Simon!"

The two then explained to them what had happened

*on the road, and how they had recognized the Lord
when he broke the bread.*

LUKE 24:13–38

J ESUS SEEMS TO have enjoyed surprising people. Consider the two followers walking on the road to Emmaus. Some authors think they were a couple, perhaps even young lovers. Others think they were running away from the dangerous situation for the followers of Jesus in Jerusalem. They are talking heatedly and sorrowfully about Jesus' death. Then suddenly Jesus is walking with them, only they don't recognize him. Immediately we begin to wonder why they didn't recognize him. Earlier in the day Mary of Magdala had recognized him. We conclude that he's deliberately hiding, perhaps disguising himself so they won't recognize him. What's this all about? Why does he join their discussion and explain why it was necessary for Jesus to die? Why doesn't he permit them to recognize him? What's going on?

All right, he wants to explain to them why it was necessary for Jesus to die. Fair enough, perhaps they're entitled to such an explanation. But why does he play the game of being a stranger? Why is it necessary for them to recognize him only "in the breaking of the bread"? Why did he give the impression he was going to walk on, to be stopped only by their pleas to "stay with us, sir"?

The only answer seems to be that he wants to enhance their surprise. Their hearts were pounding while he talked to them, but it did not occur to them to suspect who he was, even though his exegesis of the Scriptures must have been somewhat familiar to them. Only when he broke the bread (the Eucharist in some early form?) did they recognize him and then he disappeared. Again one asks, why the game? He must have felt close to this couple, loved them deeply, otherwise why single them out for an encounter on the road? Yet why delay the self-revelation until after he had instructed them?

The answer is that he wanted to surprise them, much like we want to surprise a loved one when we plan a surprise party. Moreover, they would not have heard his words of explanation in the excitement of recognizing him. They were delighted by the surprise and, I argue as the main theme of this meditation, so was Jesus. They surely would never have forgotten their encounter on the hot, dusty road outside of Jerusalem, but now they had a story to tell—in elaborate detail doubtless as time went on—with a surprise ending, the kind of ending that Jesus usually provided to his own stories. We can imagine that others who heard the story in the hours and days afterward would have nodded and said, "That's just like him. He loved to surprise us."

Resurrections are, in the nature of things, surprising events. Yet can we not say that Jesus orchestrated that axial day in human history to maximize the surprise? The women who went to the tomb early in the morning on the first day of the week found an empty tomb and an angel waiting for them. Go tell his followers that he has risen, he is not here. The other women, surprised we might imagine, out of their minds, run to tell Peter and the others. Mary of Magdala waits in the garden near the tomb, frantic with anxiety. Jesus surprises her with the tender word "Mary" (I will discuss later the extraordinary quality of Jesus' relationship with women). She clings to him for fear that he will be lost again and he gently suggests that she shouldn't worry. He's not going away yet.

Mary follows the other women and reports to the skeptical disciples what has happened. Characteristically—and perhaps chauvinistically—they dismiss her report. The dead do not rise, right? Everyone knows that women are emotional, right? Everyone knows that Mary has a crush on Jesus, right?

She leaves, frustrated perhaps by their skepticism. But Peter and John rush to the tomb to see for themselves. They find that it is empty, the burial garments neatly folded, and the waiting angel, perhaps bored by now, who tells them that Jesus isn't there anymore. They rush back to report the astonishing facts to the community. They encounter the same skepticism as Mary had, skepticism now mixed with fear. The Sanhedrin and the Romans thought they had solved their Jesus of Nazareth problem. They had not found it necessary to round up his followers and scourge them too. If, however, these crazy rumors continued they might take drastic action to stamp out the tattered remnants of the Jesus movement. Then Jesus barged in, standing suddenly in the midst of them, and suggested that they calm down, "peace."

There surely would have been other ways in which he could have revealed himself to them that would have been more orderly, more restrained, less emotional, less spectacular. And less surprising. But like his Father-in-Heaven who launched the cosmos into existence with a spectacular bang, Jesus did not believe in laid-back surprises, low-key revelations, modest demonstrations that life was stronger than death. Rather he let the expectations build up, the tensions reach a fever pitch, fear, skepticism, and joy mingle in a dangerous emotional cocktail and then, quite dramatically, proclaim peace.

A southern Baptist archaeologist at a southern university told me once that there was a phrase in the Gospels that seemed to suggest Jesus was familiar with Greek drama. He pointed out that there was certainly a theater at the Roman town of Sepphoris, within walking distance from Nazareth. However, he was convinced that Jesus, good observant Jew that he was, would never have attended such a pagan place. I was skeptical about that. Jesus was hardly uptight about the rigidities of the Law. However, Jesus certainly had a dramatic flair in which, I suspect, he delighted, especially when he was revealing good news, very good news indeed. You don't proclaim the best news ever—life is stronger than death—in a whisper.

Some folk are uneasy about the apparent contradiction in the various resurrection stories. Surely the followers of Jesus could have organized their resurrection traditions in a more systematic way so that they would be consistent, one with another. But they didn't. What was the matter with them?

I find the stories credible because of their inconsistency. Brain science teaches us that humans remember the gist of a situation quite well, but forget the details. The traditions of the various encounters with Jesus were passed on and quickly written down. The authors of the Gospels put them together without any concern about consistency. They believed that Jesus had risen and saw no point in trying to persuade others by imposing a coherence on the traditions that would have been patently artificial. Rather they included them in their stories as they perceived them, rich and powerful, if not always coherent with one another. How many people who survived the World Trade Center tragedy worry about the coherence of their accounts with those of other survivors?

The honest confusions of the stories all suggest that the various storytellers had the gist of the story—Jesus was still alive and it was the greatest surprise ever. This book will be about the stories of Jesus, the ones Jesus told, especially the parables, and the stories about him, both of which ended with surprise.

At this point I should make clear where I am coming from. I am a Catholic Christian, indeed a priest, I believe in all the Church's teachings about Jesus. I believe that in him humanity and divinity are seamlessly shared, true God and true man. I believe in the virginal conception of Jesus and his physical resurrection. I've never seen the point in trying to water down the wonderful or the surprising in the Jesus story merely to win over those who do not believe by saying, in effect, "We are not really as outrageous as we seem." I figure that if God is going to intervene in the human condition for a decisive event, he will do it big time. If God intends this intervention to be a surprise then he will make it a big surprise. It is, after all, God's cosmos. He who launched the Big Bang can rearrange things slightly when something truly decisive is about to happen. Thus the question did Jesus rise from the dead "physically" or "spiritually" has always seemed to me to be absurd. He rose. Period. Paragraph. End of revelation.

Those who argue like Bishop Spong that the Resurrection was in fact a change in the personalities and perceptions of the apostles are willing to give away the whole game because scientists say that a resurrection is impossible. But one will not win scientists to the cause of Jesus by watering down the traditional Christian conviction that the surprise of Easter Sunday was something vast, spectacular, unparalleled. My friends Hans Kung and the late Ray Brown argued once at a meeting of theologians whether a TV camera would have recorded Jesus emerging from the tomb. I couldn't see the point in the argument and still can't. Jesus was alive again and not just in the minds of his followers. The Resurrection was not just a religious experience among the apostles who were not at the time disposed to religious experiences but rather overcome with fear and grief—like Cleopas and friend scurrying away to Emmaus. The surprise of Easter surely caused a religious experience that persists even to this day. It is not a result of one.

In this context I must also comment on the charge that I hear frequently from young people that we cannot prove that Jesus ever existed. This is an old argument from atheists that apparently spreads on college campuses by word of mouth—from fellow students, teaching assistants, and professors. One must ask what kind of proof these skeptics would demand—a birth or death certificate, a transcript of grades, a feature story in the *New York Times Magazine,* a

cover story in *Time,* a long biography? Photographs, paint-
ings? Such proof was not available for anyone until recent
centuries. Eyewitness accounts of his words and deeds?

The early Christians began to write about Jesus within a
decade of his departure from earth, most notably in the
early writings of St. Paul, who claimed he encountered Jesus personally after the Resurrection and knew many of
the people who knew Jesus before the Resurrection. We
must resist the temptation to think that because the Pauline
Epistles appear in the Scriptures after the Gospels, they
are older than the Gospels. Quite the contrary, the early
epistles—Galatians, Thessalonians—portray a movement
in the very early years of its development.

They also wrote down the stories that were appearing in
the oral traditions composed by those who had known Jesus and seen his deeds and heard his words. These frag-
ments floated around from one early Christian community
to another and were the sources for the written Gospels
that appeared in the late middle of the second century.
While the various Gospels had different origins, different
emphases, and somewhat different purposes, they are all
about one complex, unpredictable, and powerfully charismatic man. None of them were written to prove that he
had lived—that would have seemed to the writers to be a
foolish question. Of course he had walked the hills of
Galilee and the streets of Jerusalem. The real issue was—
then and now—who he was. These diverse but powerful
traditions about him, scarcely a half century after his
death—the time that separates us from John Kennedy—
demonstrate the absurdity of the contention that he never

lived. And the very diversity of the four Gospels precludes the possibility that they all result from a great conspiracy to prove that a fantastical person was real. He was, as I am arguing, a vibrant, unpredictable, and surprising person. But certainly real.

I state these convictions because I do not want to argue about them. They are unrelated to my theme of surprise in the stories of Jesus and the stories about him.

One must in the Christian tradition steer a careful journey in the "True God/True Man" mystery. Simplifiers that we humans are, we try to explain the mystery in such a way as to destroy it. Or we emphasize one component of Jesus to the exclusion of the other. In the Christological conflicts of the early Church some of the emphasis may have strayed in the direction of denying the human in Jesus. More recently there has been a similar tendency among more conservative and hyper-orthodox Catholics to be nervous in the presence of the humanity of Jesus.

When I was in parish work forty years ago, our parish was visited the week after Easter by an ambitious and arrogant young bureaucrat who was investigating allegations that strange doctrines had been preached on Easter Sunday. The pastor held all of us guilty until we proved ourselves innocent. It developed that one of us had quoted the angel as saying, "You seek the man Jesus, he is no longer here." We had called Jesus a man!

I pointed out to the pastor that this was the text in the Confraternity edition of the New Testament from which the Sunday Gospel readings were taken, that it had been approved by the Bishops of the United States, and that to

deny that Jesus was a man was to be guilty of the Mono-
physite heresy. The bureaucrat huffed and warned us
about the dangers of shocking the laity and departed on his
journey to become a cardinal in another diocese.

I also assume that the New Testament is an appropriate
source for the stories and behavior of Jesus. For a hundred
and fifty years there has been a "search for the historical Jesus," an ultimately bootless attempt to get beyond the accre-
tions to Jesus' story imposed by "the Church," (often it
seems as part of a conspiracy) which is a barrier to learning
who Jesus really was and what he really believed. The most
recent manifestation of that search is the "Jesus Seminar," a
group of scholars who gather every year and vote on which
passages of the Gospels must be excised as "unauthentic."
These meetings are usually marked by public relations
hype that deeply troubles ordinary folk who don't understand that most other scholars, at least equally reputable,
ridicule this process. My response is rather different. When
one strips away much of the gospel, the Jesus who remains
is still Jesus. Professor Robert Funk, whom I quote at the beginning of this meditation, the guiding spirit of the Jesus
Seminar, has produced a description of the skeleton of the
Gospels composed only of stories and proverbs about whose
origin with the historical Jesus there can be no doubt.
Fine, I said to myself when I read it, this is a sketch of the
same Jesus as in the Gospels, the Jesus of big surprises. Indeed, Professor Funk's work on the parables has had a major influence on my reflections about the parables.

I emphasize that my meditations on the stories of Jesus—
those he told and those the early Church told about him—are

my own and hence personal and not official. Moreover, they are meditative and homiletic, not scholarly. Finally, I do not want to separate the stories told by Jesus from the rest of the Gospels, any more than the Church wants to do that when it presents story after story in its Sunday Gospel. I merely want to emphasize that the parables are the closest thing we have to a record of Jesus' experience of the Father-in-Heaven—his images of what God is like.*

The men who wrote the Gospels had various sources of the tradition available to them. These sources—oral but mostly, by the time they began to work, written down—had been shaped over time by the experiences of the Christian communities, theological reflections, mystical insights (particularly St. John's Gospel), attempts at clarification, embarrassment over some of the odd things Jesus said and did, and attempts to keep the Roman Empire at bay.

Since the search for the historical Jesus began, various forms of "criticism" endeavored to free up the real Jesus—form criticism, redaction criticism, literary criticism, and more recently narrative criticism. I have dutifully pursued these various efforts during my life as a priest and have found them very helpful in understanding the Gospels but adding relatively little to the picture of Jesus one finds in the New Testament.

The most recent criticism is called narrative-spiritual

---

* Father John Donahue S.J. has presented an excellent scholarly study of the integration of the parables into the Gospels. *The Gospel in Parable, Metaphor, Narrative and Theology in the Synoptic Gospels.* Minneapolis, Minnesota: Fortress Press, 1988.

criticism and emphasizes the importance of the story, whether it be an individual story or the whole Gospel, and the spiritual enlightenment disclosed by the story. My friend John Shea has introduced me to this approach to the New Testament and practices it with great skill in his commentaries on the Sunday Gospels. Narrative criticism takes all the disparate parts that earlier exegesis has pulled apart in the Gospels and, understanding each of the parts better, feels free to return to the whole story and to learn what it is about. As Shea has said, a story does not indoctrinate or educate, it rather invites the reader (hearer) into the world of the story so that s/he will emerge from the story with an enhanced view of the possibilities of human life.

Jesus was not the kind of man who could be hidden effectively by later generations of his followers. Moreover, though he sometimes was embarrassing (as in the parable of the indulgent judge that we will consider in a subsequent chapter) they did not want to hide him. I have often thought that in the attempt to break through the barriers that "the Church" had established to hide the real Jesus, the critics, perhaps unconsciously, were actually Protestants continuing the Reformation against the Catholic Church that had claimed an unfair advantage of a monopoly on Jesus.

Jesus is in fact indestructible. "The Church" couldn't hide him even if it tried. The critics could not reduce him to a moral teacher (as some of them thought they did) even if they tried. The Islamic version of Jesus is the same Jesus as the one in the New Testament. Islam may have a different theological explanation for him, but it's the same man they present—a man who disconcerts, challenges, surprises. (See *The Muslim Jesus: Sayings and Stories in Islamic Literature* by Tarif Khalidi, 2001.) The Jesuchristo/Sanpietro stories of Mexican folklore depict the same person. Thus the reader may trust the sensibility of the New Testament writers in the stories around which I propose to develop this meditation.

There are adversaries to my story about Jesus' stories:

1. Authors like Dan Brown and Nikos Kazantzakis (and in the films of Ron Howard and Martin Scorsese) who depict a Jesus utterly different from the one in the New Testament.
2. Popular media presentations as *Jesus Christ Superstar* and books by liberal Protestants who reduce him to a comfortable if confused moral teacher.
3. Some conservative Christians who would rather pull proof texts from Jesus out of context to support their own causes.
4. Mel Gibson whose *The Passion of the Christ* focuses obsessively, even voyeuristically, on the physical sufferings of Jesus and ignores his public life, both the stories he told and stories we are told about him.

I will not attempt to present a Christology in this meditation, to explain how the human and divine are combined in Jesus. We need a good Christology to preach to the faithful, not to explain the mystery but to propound it. However, I know of no theology books that do so without obfuscating the situation even more, especially theology books written by German theologians.

Finally I am not proposing a psychological study of Jesus, an examination of his self-consciousness as his life progressed. He had, I insist, an absolute certainty that the Father-in-Heaven would vindicate him, whether he knew exactly how that would happen I don't know and I think no one else does either. Attempts to penetrate the psychology of any public figure is a form of mind rape, even when it is done by a distinguished author. Jesus should be left to his own emotional privacy.

How did he know that the Father-in-Heaven would vindicate him? He knew because he knew the Father, the God of surprises whom he had come to tell humankind about. Thus my meditations on the stories of Jesus are also a meditation on this God of surprises about whom Jesus had come to tell us. The creator of the universe might not be a God of surprises, but anyone who argues that he is not does not know the universe and does not comprehend that a God who does not surprise is no God at all.

I apologize to the reader for taking so much time to stake out the ground on which I stand. But it is necessary that I be clear about my perspective. I'm a priest and a storyteller and a sociologist. I write about Jesus and his surprises because they reflect why Jesus came. His Father-in-Heaven was beyond doubt a God of surprises. And also a storyteller God.

Jesus the Jew

※

JESUS WAS NOT a Christian.
Nor was he Catholic.
He was a Jew.
In fact, he was a Galilean Jew.
To understand him, we must know what that means.

> Then Jesus returned to Galilee, and the power of the
> Holy Spirit was with him. The news about him spread
> throughout all that territory. He taught in the syna-
> gogues and was praised by everyone.
>
> Then Jesus went to Nazareth, where he had been
> brought up, and on the Sabbath he went as usual to the
> synagogue. He stood up to read the Scriptures and was
> handed the book of the prophet Isaiah. He unrolled
> the scroll and found the place where it is written.

> The Spirit of the Lord is upon me,
> because he has chosen me to
> bring good news to the poor.

He has sent me to proclaim liberty to the
   captives
and recovery of sight to the blind,
to set free the oppressed
and announce that the time has come
when the Lord will save his people.

Jesus rolled up the scroll, gave it back to the attendant, and sat down. All the people in the synagogue had their eyes fixed on him, as he said to them, "This passage of Scripture has come true today, as you heard it being read."

They were all well impressed with him and marveled at the eloquent words that he spoke. They said, "Isn't he the son of Joseph?"

He said to them, "I am sure that you will quote this proverb to me, 'Doctor, heal yourself.' You will also tell me to do here in my hometown the same things you heard were done in Capernaum. I tell you this," Jesus added, "A prophet is never welcomed in his hometown.

"Listen to me: It is true that there were many widows in Israel during the time of Elijah, when there was no rain for three and a half years and a severe famine spread throughout the whole land. Yet Elijah was not sent to anyone in Israel, but only to a widow living in Zarephath in the territory of Sidon. And there were many people suffering from a dreaded skin disease who lived in Israel during the time of the prophet Elijah; yet not one of them was healed, but only Naaman the Syrian."

When the people in the synagogue heard this, they were filled with anger. They rose up, dragged Jesus out of town, and took him to the top of the hill on which their town was built. They meant to throw him over the cliff, but he walked through the middle of the crowd and went his way.

LUKE 4:14–30

Jesus begins his official public life with two big surprises: he quotes from the collection of works that are attributed to the prophet Isaiah and then he applies the themes of the prophet's work to himself.

What had he been doing in the years between the incident in the temple and the showdown in the synagogue at Nazareth? We know very little about these silent years, but we can make some educated guesses. He learned how to read because he was able to read the passage from the Bible. He had studied the Scriptures, most likely backward and forward, up and down, in and out, so he was able to argue with the most distinguished of the doctors of the Law. Moreover, he had probably studied with a mentor, a rabbi with whom he could discuss and argue about the meaning of the Torah and the Law. It would be wonderful if we knew who that rabbi was because he was doubtless a dissident, perhaps because he was a member of one of the small communities that dissented from the temple priests and lawyers and also from the various schools of the Pharisees. More likely, however, he was some kind of independent practitioner, a man whose opinions and perspectives were profoundly radical and similar to the inclinations of

Jesus—which were profoundly different from other theories that existed in the seething religious pluralism of the time. In all probability the themes Jesus announced in the synagogue at Nazareth on that fateful day were the primary fruits of his years of study. Or in the terms of this meditation they were the story he proposed to tell.

Jesus announces the theme of his public life in the synagogue of his own town. Already there are surprises. Why does he start in Nazareth? Why doesn't he go to Capernaum, a bigger and more important town down on the coast of the Sea of Galilee? Does he not know that he will likely be tossed out of town in Nazareth? Why doesn't he go north to the seaport of Tyre whence his message of the kingdom of God—the sudden and decisive entrance of God into human events, and the God of Genesis and Isaiah at that—will quickly spread around the Mediterranean world? Why not go to Jerusalem, the Holy City of Judaism? Why the reliance on Isaiah of all people? What's going on?

I will not argue in this meditation about whether a given story about Jesus is "authentic"—that is whether it relates to something that actually happened or whether it is a story made up later by those who created the tradition to encode a teaching of Jesus. This one is so bizarre that it almost certainly belongs in the prior category. For my purposes it is enough that a story reflects the astonishment of the early Christians about Jesus' predilection for surprises.

If you're a Galilean, Jesus seems to think, and you intend to transform the world, you might just as well start in Galilee. So what if people doubt that anything good comes from this frontier province with its reputation for banditry and rebellion and inadequate obedience to the required observance of Jewish religion. The kingdom of God is so powerful that it can grow rapidly from anywhere in the world. Why not Nazareth?

The northern boundaries of Israel had always been amorphous. The tribe of Dan, which was supposed to have laid firm claim to those lands, had taken up fishing and commerce, it was alleged, just like the Phoenicians. The various waves of invaders that beset Israel normally came from the north. When the invaders fell back, the Jews struggled to reclaim the land, but their hold was usually tenuous and pagans tended to filter into the land and establish their own settlements. The Hasmonean kings, descendants of the Maccabees, who ruled from 164 B.C. to 37 B.C., having driven out the Syrians under Antiochus IV, tried to extend the rule of their new Jewish kingdom over the whole land of Israel. Settlers moved north into Galilee in large numbers. That land was well suited for intensive farming by small landholders because the land was fertile and streams and springs draining down from Mount Hermon in good weather provided plenty of water.

The peasants unfortunately were at the mercy of the civil rulers, Romans in Jesus' time, who taxed them heavily for the constructions of new cities like Tiberias and Sepphoris and Caesarea, and of the religious leaders in Jerusalem, who demanded their tithes for the support of the temple. The hardworking farmers could get by unless the weather was bad and their crops failed. Then they might lose their land. Some of the dispossessed became brigands and tried to rob their oppressors or anyone else who was available. They often merged with political and religious rebels called the Zealots who were determined to imitate the Maccabees and throw off the yoke of Rome just as Judas Maccabaeus had driven out the Syrians. When the final revolutions against Rome occurred, the Galileans were deeply involved. They deserved their reputation for fierce recklessness in battle.

There have been efforts to prove that Jesus was a Zealot, but they don't seem to work. Following the example of his mentor John the Baptist, he lived an ascetic life, though not as rigorous as John's. He condemned the rich who exploited the poor, but he was friendly with tax collectors (and one of them was an apostle). He was a pious Jew, but he had his own critical reading of the Scriptures and denounced the hypocrisy and corruption of Jewish leaders. The immediate cause of his arrest was his disruption of the temple, apparently a sign that he did not think the religious atmosphere of the temple was an accurate reflection of the Jewish heritage.* Was Jesus a revolutionary? Indeed yes, but a religious revolutionary driven by a vision of universal peace and justice that he called "the kingdom of heaven," a vision he had learned from his study of Isaiah.

It would appear that Galilee was relatively peaceful, though still restless, in the time of Jesus. It was a border country with a mix of religions and ethnic groups in their own enclaves. Sometimes the Arizonan in me inclines me to offer Tombstone as a contemporary metaphor, though Capernaum, a prosperous fishing village on the Sea of Galilee,

---

* I have often wondered how he would react to the contemporary Vatican.

was not as dangerous as Tombstone was in the era of the Earps and the Clantons.

Herod the Great had replaced the Hasmoneans with his own dynasty and built a splendid new temple in Jerusalem. His sons had minor government positions in various regions. A Roman prefect in Judea kept an eye on the whole region. Rome was in control but only tenuously—and brutally.

Jesus' vision was quite different from that of the political revolutionaries. His vision was of a kingdom of heaven rooted in the world view of Isaiah and Daniel—apparently his favorite books in the Scriptures. Isaiah is an extremely complicated book, divided by most commentators into three separate books though with common themes. Moreover, even within chapters there are different voices speaking.

The mystical vision of Isaiah is summarized in several verses at the beginning of the second chapter of the book:

> *In days to come, the mountain of the Lord's house shall be established in the highest mountain and raised above all the hills. All nations shall stream toward it, many peoples shall come and say, "Come let us go to the Lord's mountain that he may instruct us in his ways and we may walk in his paths."*
>
> *For from Zion shall go forth instruction and the word of the Lord from Jerusalem.*

It would not be a military kingdom, but a reign of peace. It would not be exclusively Jewish, because the nations would come as nations. The God of Zion, presumably a

Jewish monopoly, would now become the God of all nations and peoples.

It would be a kingdom centered in Mount Zion, but perhaps only a symbolic Zion, open to all the nations and peoples of the world, and served by a band of servants like those described in the "Third" book of Isaiah, or the *maskilim* ("men proficient in wisdom") of Daniel and animated by his vision of the Father-in-Heaven about whom Jesus told his stories. Justification for this universal vision could certainly be found in the Scriptures and was celebrated by some of the dissident religious groups (those who were independent of the temple and the Jewish authorities) like the Essenes who gathered at the Wadi Qumran near the Dead Sea (in whose ruins the famous Dead Sea Scrolls were found). Jesus, however, saw much more in Isaiah than any of his contemporaries, so much more that his vision was qualitatively different.

Jesus was a devout Jew, but he did not accept all the minute rigorous interpretations of the scribes in Jerusalem. Quite the contrary, he denounced both the rules of the rabbis and the exactions of the temple priests. While I believe that Jesus had a mentor, the only other influence on him was John the Baptist, whose ascetic lifestyle he continued to imitate. If his Judaism was different from that of Jerusalem it is even more different from the tradition of Rabbinic Judaism that emerged after the fall of Jerusalem. One should not evaluate the Judaism of Jesus by his deviations from Jewish rules articulated later. Second Temple Judaism was a "blooming buzzing pluralism" that had yet to take on more detailed and more exclusive formulae. Jesus' convictions about the kingdom of God was an authentic component of that pluralism. Strictly speaking, Jesus was not a rabbi. He was not old enough, unmarried, and had no distinguished teachers. His freedom to make the imagery of Isaiah and Daniel his own was almost certainly facilitated by the amorphous and often chaotic religious and political situation in Galilee. His only credentials were his personal authority, the miracles he worked, and the stories he told.

He believed that a new era was beginning, an era that he called the kingdom of heaven, in which there would be justice and peace supported by the God of creation, an incredibly loving and forgiving God. This kingdom of heaven already existed in his own preaching and would expand and flourish like the mustard seed that turns into a tree. His followers, like those of Isaiah and Daniel, would continue his work.

This vision was profoundly Jewish and showed a deep understanding of the relevant Scriptures—astonishing in one without any formal education in the Scriptures. It was also profoundly Galilean in his willingness to recast the tradition to fit more closely with the realities of ordinary life in Galilee and his own experience of the Father. Jesus lived and died a Jew, indeed an orthodox Jew (small "o"), though, like many others of his time, he was somewhat dissident. To label him an apostate, as some contemporary Jewish writers do, is to fail to understand the great variety and diversity of Judaism at the time of the Second Temple.

Was the mystical, eschatological vision of Isaiah especially appealing to Jesus because it explicitly included Galilee in the new Zion? And because it was pluralistic and also included the others who lived in and around its border regions? And because it fit the environment and history of Jesus' little world? Did Jesus have to be a Galilean to find the kingdom of God envisioned by Isaiah (and Daniel) an especially appropriate organizing symbol for his stories of the Father-in-Heaven? Was it therefore relatively easy for Jesus to embrace this out-of-the-mainstream element in the Jewish religious worldview?

Note carefully how Jesus reacted to the skepticism of his fellow townsmen. They had no problem with his invocation of Isaiah, not even his outlandish claim that in him the vision of Isaiah was fulfilled. They complained rather that Jesus had not worked any miracles in Nazareth. And who did he think he was anyway? Rather than back off and hedge his claim, he told them that the kingdom of God's love extended even to the gentiles like the Sidonite widow of Zarephath and the Syrian Naaman. That the kingdom of heaven would include Galileans was not disturbing to the townsfolk of Nazareth. However, it was not only surprising but infuriating that he seemed willing at the very beginning to invoke Isaiah to legitimatize the presence of Syrians and Phoenicians in the kingdom. No wonder they wanted to throw him over the edge of the cliff.

In the Jewish religious heritage there had always been (and there still are) strains of both universalism and particularism. The Holy One was indeed the God of all the nations, but he was also the special and particular God of the Jewish people. He was jealous of them and they were jealous of him. In practice that meant that the gentiles were despised. How dare the goy claim the Jewish God as their own—unless they were willing to be circumcised and honor the rules of the Jewish law?

Jesus refused to accept such a narrow depiction of his Father-in-Heaven. The Father was the loving God of everyone. Such an idea was as profoundly offensive to most Jews of his time as it was to his fellow Nazarenes. It was not right, they would have thought, that someone push the universalism of Isaiah that far. My friend Jacob Neusner once remarked to me that Jesus and St. Paul understood the universalism of the Jewish heritage better than most of their contemporaries. Better, I would add, than most Jews today—and most gentiles too. That first interlude in Nazareth hinted at the troubles he would face for the rest of his mission. He was both too popular and too heretical. The synagogue at Nazareth was a paradigm for the rest of his public life.

Human religion oscillates between the particular and universal, between Galilee and Jerusalem, between the neighborhood and the world. The particular cannot exist perhaps without the universal, the neighborhood without the world. But the opposite is not the case. The world needs the concrete particularity of the neighborhood if the religious vision is not to be like the seed that falls on hard ground and withers and dies because it has not been able to sink its roots into the earth. The kingdom of heaven that Jesus saw as emerging in that synagogue at Nazareth required that he be a Jew. It also required that he be a Jew from the borderlands of Galilee of the gentiles. Yet despite his global vision, he preached mostly to Jewish peasants and avoided the rich Roman cities and the powerful

Phoenician ports. It was yet another surprise that he insisted on deep particularistic roots as a precondition for a universalistic mission. While he indeed traveled in the gentile lands around Galilee, he avoided the powerful and influential cities in the regions across the Jordan and in Phoenicia. How was his mustard seed to grow and spread with such a limited audience? Moreover, his band of brothers were peasants and fishermen from Galilee, undistinguished losers at best. With such a limited expanse of his mission and such ineffectual disciples—who did not understand in the slightest what he was talking about—how could he hope to preach the kingdom of heaven to all the nations that would share in the eschatological dream of Isaiah? One would have said that without his charisma and authority there was no reason to think that his imagination of the kingdom of heaven—always just about a foot over your head as a woman from County Kerry once remarked— would spread to the ends of the earth.

Yet the dream of Jesus did come true and is still coming true. His servants, his *maskilim,* never all that impressive down through history, would nonetheless keep that dream alive, if at times only just barely.

Or to put the matter differently, how many of those who drove him out of the synagogue would have expected that the story of the challenge he threw at them there would still be told two millennia later?

Now who is surprised?

Sean Freyne sees Galilee not only as the source of that dream but also as the training ground for its spread. Jesus saw himself, Freyne suggests, as both the suffering servant of Isaiah and the wise man of Daniel and that his followers understood themselves as following in the footsteps of their leader. "Going back to Galilee" after the Resurrection was neither an exercise of nostalgia nor a return to the everyday of their past lives, but a recalling of the mission and ministry that had challenged them initially in Galilee, and that was now about to make new and dangerous demands if they were to be true to the call of the rejected servant whom they believed had been exalted by God.

We have heard the story of the synagogue at Nazareth often in our lives. It is always fascinating because we delight in the folly of Jesus' neighbors, though it is our own folly too. But familiarity with it causes us to pay little attention to it. Yes, of course, Jesus applies the prophecy of Isaiah to himself. We don't realize how revolutionary that story is, how shocking it would be to most Jews of his time, and how disturbing his claim would be, even today.

Jesus and Women

❧ The Fellow Travelers ❧

*He traveled from one town and village to another,
preaching the good news of the kingdom of God. Ac-
companying him were the twelve and some women who
had been cured of evil spirits and infirmities, Mary
of Magdala, from whom seven devils had gone out,
Johanna, the wife of Herod's steward Chuza, Su-
sanna and many others who provide for them out of
their resources.*

LUKE 8:1–3

Before I turn to the stories Jesus told, I will discuss the
relationships of Jesus with women, which are the most
astonishing of the stories told about him by those who
knew him. Someone has remarked that the attitudes and
behavior of Jesus with women in his time and place are
enough by themselves to suggest that he might well be the
Son of God.

The three verses above from St. Luke's Gospel do not

initially make much of an impression as one reads them today. Yes, the apostles and the holy women traveled around
with Jesus, what is so impressive about that? But for both
Jews and gentiles of the time, it was profoundly shocking,
another of Jesus' dangerous surprises. What Jesus was doing was simply not done. Women may have ministered to
the great rabbis of the Second Temple era, but they did not
travel through the country with them. What terrible scan-
dals might come of such an arrangement? What dreadful
deeds might happen under the night sky of the desert? To
make matters worse—and this would shock the Romans
perhaps even more than the Jews—St. Luke practically
equates the women travelers with the apostles. Not only
was Jesus tolerating the inappropriate mixing of the sexes,
he also seems to be proclaiming their equality, a logical conclusion of his Isaiahan vision perhaps, but yet dangerous—
even today.

So unacceptable were such notions that the other three
evangelists do not discuss the women who were part of the
Jesus group until they stood at the foot of the cross. Luke,
however, places them not only as fellow travelers but as
those who were loyal in faith under the cross and loyal to
the buried Jesus early in the morning on the first day of the
week and thus suggests that in some ways they were superior in their faith in comparison to the apostles. Jesus took
the universalism of Isaiah very seriously indeed.

We know almost nothing about their stories. Did traditions about them exist in the early Church? Were they dis-
creetly covered up for fear of scandalizing both Jews and
gentiles? We are told only that Jesus had driven seven de-

vils out of Mary of Magdala. There are no grounds, however, for identifying her with the sinful woman who at the
home of Simon the Pharisee washed the feet of Jesus with
her tears, much less with the youthful Mary of Bethany,
the sister of Martha and Lazarus. The Christian writers of
the Middle Ages were baffled by all the women named
Mary in the stories and tried to consolidate them (but not
as part of a plot by "the Church" as Dan Brown would
have us believe). The "seven devils" do not mean that she
was a great sinner nor a prostitute, but rather a deeply
troubled woman. The only other part of her story we
know is in the moving scene between her and Jesus outside
the empty tomb—which St. Luke tells, though he must
know that it would shock the prurient among his readers.
He could never have imagined that later readers such as
Dan Brown, Nikos Kazantzakis, and Martin Scorsese
would identify her with Mary of Bethany—despite patent
evidence that they are very different women, though both
of them obviously loved Jesus and were loved by him in
return.

Did these women who traveled with Jesus find him sexually attractive? How could they not have? He must have
been a terribly impressive male—strong, handsome, serious, self-confident, brilliant, fond of surprises, a powerful
and charismatic speaker, doubtless witty when he wanted
to be—and always respectful of them. He was the kind of
man on whom women could easily form what we today
call crushes. Yet his attractiveness was not purely physical,
nor for that matter purely spiritual. Rather it was the result
of a seamless combination of the physical and the spiritual

of the presence of the Spirit radiating out of the incarnate son of God.

Moreover, he treated them with great respect and reverence as well as sensitive and gentle tenderness. He did not demean them or talk down to them or keep them in their place—whatever that place might be. For women in those days as well as today, he seems to have been everything that women admire in a man. Was there a sexual dimension to their attraction for Jesus? How could there not have been? Women could not deny their sexual emotions, though it does not follow they were doomed to act on them, especially if they received no hint that Jesus expected such behavior or would even tolerate it.

Was Jesus sexually attracted to women? Did he feel sexual desire for some of them? One can answer "no" to that question only if one wants to deny the humanity of Jesus or argue that sexual feelings are in themselves evil—which many Christians today would still want to argue. Jesus was not sexless, he was not a eunuch. He had the same hormones as do all male humans.

Nor in principle would he have been any less the Chosen One of God if he had married and fathered children. Kazantzakis (and Scorsese) would have us believe that the last temptation of Jesus was to accept married domesticity and give up his mission. But married love and sexual pleasure between spouses are good and not to be condemned. All we can demand of Jesus because of who and what he was would be that he never exploit a woman or a woman's love. Jesus indeed had hormones, but because he was who he was, he focused his sexual energies on the task of announcing the kingdom of God. Dan Brown and Ron Howard would have us believe that he married Mary of Magdala and that they had a daughter they called Sarah. Many defenders of the traditional Christian faith call this allegation blasphemous. In fact, there is no evidence that it was true, but if Jesus did not marry, the reason was not that he could not marry, but that he chose not to marry. As a true man in all things, sin alone excepted, he could imagine married intimacy and sexual love with a woman and enjoy those images. Those who believe that Jesus' celibacy was not optional skate dangerously close to Docetism, the heresy that said that Jesus only appeared to be human. An allegation that Jesus was married is false. However to dismiss it as blasphemy is offensive to pious ears and smells of heresy (as the medieval theologians might say).

Celibacy was rare in the era of Second Temple Judaism, but not unknown. However, it was generally expected of Jewish men that they marry, indeed one could not become a rabbi until after one was married. For Jesus to have a wife would have surprised no one. Quite the contrary, as a rabbi it would have been expected of him. There would have been no need to keep it a secret. Indeed to be married would have been more acceptable than to travel around the country with a mixed group of men and women. We hear nothing of Jesus' wife because there was no wife—and this long before the Church began to endorse celibacy. Jesus, we must assume, must have sent unmistakable signals—a mixture perhaps of affection and dignity—to women that while he liked women, indeed delighted in them, he had other concerns in his life. Jesus was different and it would seem that his followers came to take his difference for granted. Even his mother seemed to understand that.

It has been argued that Jesus did not ordain any of these women as priests at the last supper because they were not present. This is a hyper-literalist interpretation of the emergence of the sacraments. However, whatever one may say about the issue of the ordination of women, how do we know they weren't at the last supper? Who did the cooking and who cleaned up afterward?

❧ *The Mother* ☙

There was a wedding in the town of Cana in Galilee. Jesus' mother was there, and Jesus and his disciples had also been invited to the wedding. When the wine had given out, Jesus' mother said to him, "They are out of wine."

"You must not tell me what to do," Jesus replied. "My time has not yet come."

Jesus' mother then told the servants, "Do whatever he tells you."

The Jews have rules about ritual washing, and for this purpose six stone water jars were there, each one large enough to hold between twenty and thirty gallons. Jesus said to the servants, "Fill these jars with water." They filled them to the brim, and then he told them, "Now draw some water out and take it to the man in charge of the feast." They took him the water, which now had turned into wine, and he tasted it. He did not know where this wine had come from (but, of course, the servants who had drawn out the water knew); so he called the bridegroom and said to him, "Everyone else serves the best wine first, and after the guests have drunk a lot, he serves the ordinary wine. But you have kept the best wine until now!"

Jesus performed this first miracle in Cana in Galilee; there he revealed his glory, and his disciples believed in him.

JOHN 2:1–11

The Cana story is among the most charming to be found anywhere in the Bible, and indeed in all of world literature. We find it only in St. John's Gospel, written perhaps sixty-five years after the fact. Can we credit the subtle and witty exchange between Jesus and his mother? Or do we have an ingeniously crafted tale, dense with Johannine mystical allusions? Whoever wrote the stories that are included in the Fourth Gospel was a brilliant teller of tales. I believe that John or his storyteller found the Cana interlude in one of the traditions available to him and then retold it with the comic irony that it now exhibits. There must have been a memory of an incident at Cana on which the tradition perhaps elaborated. More to the point the story recounts what Jesus was like, and his mother, and how they related to one another; memories that the early Christians surely treasured. What matters, then, is not the provenance of the story nor the various meanings, but the richness of the story itself.

In an era when there were no films, no television, no

radio, no computer games, weddings were one of the few available sources for entertainment for the peasant farmers of Palestine. They lasted for a week and were at least as lively as Jewish weddings today—singing, dancing, eating, drinking, talking, telling tales, gossiping, remembering. The bride and groom would go off to another room or behind a protective curtain to consummate their marriage and the dancing and the music and the celebrating would continue. I like to think that they ran out of wine because the hosts did not expect Jesus to show up with his apostles. Thus his mother may have had a tone of mild reproach in her voice when she reported that there was no wine. You bring your thirsty young friends here and look what happens.

A lot of theological ink has been spilled about what Jesus meant in his response to her. The ink, I think, is wasted. The point of the story—indeed the delight of the story—is what Mary did immediately. The servants must have been astonished at the nerve of this woman. What right did she have to tell them what to do. Yet she spoke with sufficient authority that they did what she told them to do, even if it meant pouring a lot of scarce water into the big ritual containers— one hundred eighty gallons of it. Again he spoke with authority like that of his mother, so they filled the water jars.

One hundred eighty gallons of the best wine! How could the guests possibly consume it! What did the hosts do with it afterward! Were there other parties in the weeks ahead before it turned sour! We do not know, though it is fun to speculate. Jesus, however, had staged an astonishing surprise so that a wedding party would not be a flop, so that the young couple and their parents would not be embarrassed, and so that the feast at Cana would be remembered for a long time in Galilee, even if had not eventually found its way into St. John's Gospel.

How delighted Mary must have been in the grace of her son, though perhaps she wasn't so surprised because she knew him very well. It does not seem odd to assume that Jesus' relationship with women was modeled on his relationship with his mother.

The huge amount of wine was excessive. Why not just one water jar? Jesus liked being excessive, just as his Father-in-Heaven was excessive. Why so many stars? Why not just one galaxy?

❧ *The Sisters in Bethany* ❧

As they continued their journey he entered a village where a woman whose name was Martha welcomed him. She had a sister named Mary who sat beside the Lord at his feet listening to him speak. Martha burdened with much serving came to him and said, "Lord, do you not care that my sister has left me by myself to do the serving. Tell her to help me." The Lord said to her in reply, "Martha, Martha, you are anxious and worried about many things. There is need of only one thing. Mary has chosen the better part and it will not be taken from her."

LUKE 10:38–42

A man named Lazarus, who lived in Bethany, became sick. Bethany was the town where Mary and her sister Martha lived. (This Mary was the one who poured the perfume on the Lord's feet and wiped them with her hair; it was her brother Lazarus who was sick.) The sisters sent Jesus a message: "Lord, your dear friend is sick."

When Jesus heard it, he said, "The final result of this sickness will not be the death of Lazarus; this has happened in order to bring glory to God, and it will be the means by which the Son of God will receive glory."

Jesus loved Martha and her sister and Lazarus. Yet when he received the news that Lazarus was sick, he stayed where he was for two more days. Then he said to the disciples, "Let us go back to Judea."

"Teacher," the disciples answered, "just a short time ago the people there wanted to stone you; and are you planning to go back?"

Jesus said, "A day has twelve hours, doesn't it? So whoever walks in broad daylight does not stumble, for he sees the light of this world. But if he walks during the night he stumbles, because he has no light." Jesus said this and then added, "Our friend Lazarus has fallen asleep, but I will go and wake him up."

The disciples answered, "If he is asleep, Lord, he will get well."

Jesus meant that Lazarus had died, but they thought he meant natural sleep. So Jesus told them plainly, "Lazarus is dead, but for your sake I am glad that I was not with him, so that you will believe. Let us go to him."

Thomas (called the Twin) said to his fellow disciples, "Let us all go along with the Teacher, so that we may die with him!"

When Jesus arrived, he found that Lazarus had been buried four days before. Bethany was less than two miles from Jerusalem, and many Judeans had come to see Martha and Mary to comfort them about their brother's death.

When Martha heard that Jesus was coming, she went out to meet him, but Mary stayed in the house. Martha said to Jesus, "If you had been here, Lord, my brother would not have died! But I know that even now God will give you whatever you ask him for."

"Your brother will rise to life," Jesus told her.

"I know," she replied, "that he will rise to life on the last day."

Jesus said to her, "I am the resurrection and the life. Whoever believes in me will live, even though he dies; and whoever lives and believes in me will never die. Do you believe this?"

"Yes, Lord!" she answered. "I do believe that you are the Messiah, the Son of God, who was to come into the world."

After Martha said this, she went back and called her sister Mary privately. "The Teacher is here," she told her, "and is asking for you." When Mary heard this, she got up and hurried out to meet him. (Jesus had not yet arrived in the village, but was still in the place where Martha had met him.) The people who were in the house with Mary comforting her followed her when they saw her get up and hurry out. They thought that she was going to the grave to weep there.

Mary arrived where Jesus was, and as soon as she saw him, she fell at his feet. "Lord," she said, "if you had been here, my brother would not have died!"

Jesus saw her weeping, and he saw how the people with her were weeping also; his heart was touched, and he was deeply moved. "Where have you buried him?" he asked them.

"Come and see, Lord," they answered.

Jesus wept. "See how much he loved him!" the people said.

But some of them said, "He gave sight to the blind man, didn't he? Could he not have kept Lazarus from dying?"

Deeply moved once more, Jesus went to the tomb, which was a cave with a stone place at the entrance. "Take the stone away!" Jesus ordered.

Martha, the dead man's sister, answered, "There will be a bad smell, Lord. He has been buried four days!"

Jesus said to her, "Didn't I tell you that you would see God's glory if you believed?" They took the stone away. Jesus looked up and said, "I thank you, Father, that you listen to me. I know that you always listen to me, but I say this for the sake of the people here, so that they will believe that you sent me." After he had said this, he called out in a loud voice, "Lazarus,

*come out!" He came out, his hands and feet wrapped
in grave cloths, and with a cloth around his face.
"Untie him," Jesus told them, "and let him go."*

JOHN 11:1–44

Somewhere, I am convinced, in a musty museum or an
old library or buried in the desert, perhaps in Ethiopia,
there is a catena of stories about the family at Bethany on
which both St. Luke and St. John relied in their Gospels,
stories that circulated among the early first-century Christians. Martha and Mary and Lazarus must have been well
known. Were they not a surrogate family for Jesus? Did he
not stay at their home when he was visiting Jerusalem?
Was it not there that he sought release from the tensions of
fighting with those who would destroy him in the Talmu-
dic arguments in the temple courtyards? The Gospel writers introduce them into their narratives as if we already
know who they are.

We hunger today for as many details of the life of Jesus as
we can possibly have. It is a cultural necessity in our time to
explore all the possible details of the lives of great men—
Washington, Lincoln, Jefferson. We cannot be content with
mere hints and inferences from events about which we
know few details. Thus we lament the enormous waste of
stories about Jesus that must have existed in years immediately after his return to the Father-in-Heaven. Our curios-
ity wants to know more, more, more—at least as much as
those who knew him when he was here on earth or who
heard the stories about him. I would love to know more
about Lazarus and his sisters. The sisters were not married.

In the customs of those days they would have been at most in their middle teens.* Lazarus, who doesn't have any lines, was even younger, twelve or thirteen. We hear nothing about their parents, so they had probably died. Perhaps they had been friends of Jesus who had become a substitute parent for them. The emotional ties between Jesus and the three children were therefore very strong.

They were well known in Jerusalem, socially prominent and affluent—hence Mary could purchase the expensive ointment that she would pour on the head of Jesus at his final dinner there before he went to Jerusalem to die.

If we accept that Martha and Mary were both teenagers, the squabbling between them becomes understandable. It is also not unlikely that they both had crushes on him, fragile emotions of the young that would be both volatile and shallow. Jesus handled their attractions for him with respect and dignity because he loved them both. They were "in love" with him and he loved them.

There has been much discussion about the contest between the active and contemplative lives that the Bethany sisters were supposed to represent. I think, however, that such argument misses the point that this was a family of which Jesus had become a part and in which he was deeply involved. Jesus' answer was not what most parents or surrogate parents would have said. Rather he was acting out a little parable. He was warning that a hostess ought not to

---

* It was necessary that women marry young in those days, so that they could begin to have children when they were most fertile. Infant and maternal mortality rates were so high that the survival of a people depended on early marriage and early childbearing—and accepted fatalistically early death.

be so involved in preparations that she had no time for her guests—a failing that is epidemic in the human condition. The Father-in-Heaven, he was saying, has unlimited time for all of us.

In the Middle Ages Mary of Bethany was equated with Mary of Magdala, with the sinful woman who washed the feet of Jesus with her tears, and with the woman taken in adultery (more about her later). However, her personality is obviously different from the personalities of the other women, perhaps even more vulnerable because she was just beginning to be a woman. Jesus accepted her affection and Martha's hard work. But one thing alone was necessary.

There are in these two stories about Jesus and the sisters in Bethany two surprises, the first is Jesus' defense of Mary for attending to the guests instead of the preparations for the dinner in St. Luke and then the huge surprise of Lazarus coming out of the tomb in St. John. Notice how Jesus orchestrated the surprise for its maximum impact. He was not showing off; however, he was preparing them for what would happen—the revelation of the power of the Father-in-Heaven, even over death.

For those who read the story from perspective of rigid orthodoxy, there was also the surprise that Jesus wept. He was God, was he not? He knew that Lazarus would come forth at his call. He knew that eventually Lazarus would die again as would his sisters and everyone born of women, including Jesus himself. He knew that the Father-in-Heaven would eventually vindicate him and all those who followed him. So what was there to cry about?

Berdyayev, the Russian mystic, once remarked that even

when the little baby cries God weeps. While that dictum might not survive strict theological analysis, its poetic meaning is quite clear. When we mourn, God, in ways we cannot possibly understand, somehow, some way, mourns with us. Of course Jesus cried, though he knew the outcome of the story. He cried because his close friends, in a way his children, were overcome by sadness. He cried because he realized that this sadness was an inevitable dimension of human experience. He wept for all of us.

They were not part of the company of women disciples who traveled with Jesus and were not involved at either his crucifixion or resurrection, though it seems as unlikely that he did not visit them just as it is unlikely that he did not visit his mother (even if the early Church seems to have no memory of such visits).

But was Lazarus really dead? the skeptic and the skeptic in each of us demands. Maybe he was only in a state of suspended animation. Yes, Jesus said he was dead, but maybe he did not mean *really* dead. Perhaps like the son of the widow of Naim and the daughter of Jairus, Lazarus was in a deep trance. Whatever, the body that was in the tomb came forth wrapped in his burial robes. His sisters, delirious with joy, unbound him. They doubtless promised that they would never pick on their little brother again. Most of the skeptics in the crowd cheered even though many of them refused to believe what they were seeing. The rumor of the raising of Lazarus would be cited in a few days as grounds for killing Jesus. The dead cannot rise, can they? If they appear to, it is a dangerous and frightening fraud. If they really rise, then it is a grave threat to all civil and religious authorities. So nervously we moderns (much like the contemporaries of Jesus) conclude that either what happened in that graveyard in Bethany was a fable, a story made up, or . . . or a trick, a fraud, an exercise in white or black magic. The safest reaction to the Lazarus story is to conclude that it never really happened.

One defending the reality of the miracle might say that the rich details that St. John provides suggest that he was describing a real event. However, it was at least sixty years later. We know that the writer of the Johannine stories was brilliant. As we saw in the Cana narrative he could tell an old story with characters and dialogue and make it sound like it happened last week. Maybe the storyteller had taken an old story about how Lazarus had apparently died and Jesus had revived him, as, arguably, he had revived the daughter of Jairus and the son of the widow of Naim. It was proof that Jesus had extraordinary healing powers, but not that he could bring the dead back to life.

Maybe.

Nonetheless there was a powerful memory in the tradition of the early Christians that Jesus had a close relationship with the three young people of Bethany and that he had preserved Lazarus from death. The Gospel author could not have made up the story from whole cloth and expected to get away with it. Moreover the serious Bible scholars now agree that the tradition of Jesus' miracles was too strong to have been made up and added by the later Church. What is remarkable about the stories of such miracles is how terse and restrained they are in comparison with the tales told about other thaumaturges of the time. It cannot be denied that Jesus had marvelous healing powers. To remove that fact from the New Testament, as some "liberals" wish to do, is to deprive the books of all coherence and meaning. We can speculate if we wish about the nature of those powers and we'll never understand them.

Nonetheless, the fact remains that the early Christians believed that something wonderful happened in Bethany. Wonderful and surprising. For young women he loved, after he had wept for their suffering. The point in the context of this meditation is that Jesus had topped all his previous surprises, whatever he had done and however he had done it.

❧ *Mary of Magdala—Did Jesus Love Her?* ❧

Magdala was a town on the Sea of Galilee, a few miles south of Capernaum, affluent from fishing, salting of fish, manufacture of boats and boat materials, dyeing, and making of ceramics. All of which suggest that this Mary was as affluent as Mary of Bethany.

> *Mary stayed outside the tomb weeping. And as she wept, she bent over the tomb and saw two angels sitting there, one at the head and one at the feet where the body of Jesus had been.*
>
> *And they said to her, "Woman, why are you weeping?"*
>
> *And she replied, "They have taken my Lord and I do not know where they have laid him."*

When she had said that she turned around and saw Jesus there, but she did not know that it was Jesus.

Jesus said to her, "Woman, why are you weeping? Whom are you looking for?"

She thought it was the gardener and said to him, "Sir, if you carried him away, tell me where you laid him and I will take him."

Jesus said to her, "Mary!"

She turned and said to him, "Rabboni" (which in Hebrew means "teacher").

Jesus said, "Stop holding on to me because I have not yet ascended to the father. But go to my brothers and tell them that I am going to my father and your father, to my God and your God."

Mary of Magdala went to the disciples and announced, "I have seen the Lord," and what he told her.

JOHN 20:11–18

Mary of Magdala is mentioned nine times in the New Testament, in addition to St. Luke's account of her traveling with Jesus and the other women in the company of the disciples. In all the Gospels, she stands with the other women at the foot of the cross and comes early in the morning on the first day of the week to finish the anointing of his body. The dialogue reported by St. John's always gifted storyteller are the only words she recites. In a late second-century or early third-century nine-page fragment called *The Gospel of Mary* she is depicted as participating in an obscure theological dialogue with Peter and the apostles, an incident that is utterly different from the context and the style of the four canonical Gospels. It would appear to be part of a collection of Gnostic tracts, neo-Platonist dissent from mainstream early Christianity. These materials are all that Dan Brown and others like him needed to spin a fantasy tale of her relationship with Jesus and her role in the early Church (and today). Such fantasies are so appealing in their absurdity that they will always have an appeal to those who seek secret knowledge that others don't have. Yet the little dialogue that St. John narrates, with the usual skillful details, is more wonderful than the most seductive of the Gnostic tales. Mary of Magdala, not Peter, not any of the apostles, is deputed to be the herald of the Resurrection. Moreover, she was yet another happy victim of Jesus' surprises, surprises that, as always where women were concerned, were always marked by courtesy, respect, and affection.

Did she love Jesus? How could she not have loved him? He had saved her from the emotional troubles that had paralyzed her. He was certainly the most attractive man she had ever encountered. And also the kindest, the most gentle, and the most respectful. Better to say she adored him.

And did he love her? Again one must ask how he could not have responded with love to a woman so utterly dependent on him and devoted to him. Could he have imagined the possibility of making love with her? If he were human he certainly could have and would have.

And given his total commitment to the kingdom of the Father-in-Heaven, it could not have gone any further as both he and Mary knew well. Yet their love surely had a deep impact on both their personalities. These things we can certainly say and admire their devotion to each other. Anything more than that, *pace* Dan Brown, Nikos Kazantzakis, and Martin Scorsese, is absurd fantasy. It destroys in the name of cheap thrills the beauty of that love, not the ethereal and disembodied love of the Gnostic gospels, but the deep affection between too powerful adults who knew their roles and were quite capable of sublimating physical passion in the name of the kingdom of the Father-in-Heaven. It is difficult to ignore this message in St. John's dialogue in the garden outside the tomb.

Once more Jesus delights in surprising those he loves. As with the couple on the road to Emmaus, he disguises himself. He disguises, as folk who have risen from the dead apparently can do, both his physical appearance and his voice—until he utters the word that the woman of Magdala cannot fail to understand, her own name.

A novelist would have no trouble imagining the emotions that surge through each of them, joy, love, hope, victory, renewal, the sense of a new beginning! Though I write novels, I will resist the temptation to fictionalize this passage and leave the imagination to the reader. However, I warn the reader that the love between Jesus and the woman from Magdala was not the disembodied love that a certain kind of Christian piety would like to pretend. It was rather a passionate love between two humans who knew what their destinies were.

One can easily picture the reaction of Peter and the others when Mary appeared in the upper room and told them that she had seen the Lord. They had already heard the accounts of the other women about the empty tomb. Perhaps

Peter and John had already raced to the tomb and found it empty. Now Mary of Magdala claimed to have seen him and talked to him. Perhaps they thought that Mary, like all women, was inclined to be a little unstable and to imagine things. Her grief was so powerful that she could wish to see the Lord still alive and actually think she had seen him. The tomb was empty, yes, but someone had stolen the body. Jesus was dead. He had died on the cross. The dead did not rise. Moreover if Jesus, who had revived Lazarus, somehow managed to revive himself, surely he would have reported immediately to them and not to a woman, especially this woman who tended to be a bit hysterical.

Perhaps they felt guilty because they had run away and the women in their band had remained at the foot of the cross. They might have excused themselves by the argument that the women were in no danger from the Roman authority but his male followers could easily be arrested and crucified just as Jesus had. No doubt, the Romans were always brutally thorough. Besides, they could never understand why Jesus permitted the women to travel with them. That practice gave the Scribes and Pharisees something to complain about and added very little to the effectiveness of Jesus. He didn't need them and neither did the apostles. Their financial help was useful, but that didn't give them the right to tag along. They would have contributed to Jesus anyway, even if he made them stay home where they belonged.

They didn't complain to Jesus about the women, because it was evident that he would not accept such complaints.

Just the same it was an unwise decision. Surely the master knew that women were not reliable. Hence the very fact that someone might have claimed to Mary that he was Jesus was proof that it couldn't possibly be him. Probably a Roman spy. Or an agent of the Sanhedrin.

The radical equality of everyone in the kingdom of God was an idea that was beyond their comprehension. It was absurd to think that Jesus would appear first of all to a woman and an unstable one at that—absurd and scandalous. We find it acceptable today only because the scene in the garden outside the tomb has become commonplace. We have heard it told so often on Easter morning that we take it for granted. Same story as last year. We don't notice that it is the kind of story that a radical feminist might have composed.

Yet it was one more of Jesus' surprises and this time a powerful and dangerous one. Eventually it became trite, a story one could tell without fear anyone might see astonishing implications in it. But for the early Christians it was surely embarrassing, something that they would not emphasize in their preaching. St. John, writing after the other evangelists, could not leave it out. Shocking it may have been, but just the same it had happened. It would be a long time before Christians could face the full implications of the story, if indeed they have even today.

To put it in modern terms, when Jesus chose a human to announce officially his return to life, he engaged in affirmative action and selected a woman.

❦ *A Samaritan Woman* ❦

In Samaria he came to a town named Sychar, which was not far from the field that Jacob had given to his son Joseph. Jacob's well was there, and Jesus, tired out by the trip, sat down by the well. It was about noon.

A Samaritan woman came to draw some water, and Jesus said to her, "Give me a drink of water." (His disciples had gone into town to buy food.)

The woman answered, "You are a Jew, and I am a Samaritan—so how can you ask me for a drink?" (Jews will not use the same cups and bowls that Samaritans use.)

Jesus answered, "If you only knew what God gives and who it is that is asking you for a drink, you would ask him, and he would give you life-giving water."

"Sir," the woman said, "you don't have a bucket, and the well is deep. Where would you get that life-giving water? It was our ancestor Jacob who gave us this well; he and his sons and his flocks all drank from it. You don't claim to be greater than Jacob, do you?"

Jesus answered, "Whoever drinks this water will get thirsty again but whoever drinks the water that I will give him will never be thirsty again. The water that I will give him will become in him a spring which will provide him with life-giving water and give him eternal life."

"Sir," the woman said, "give me that water! Then I

*will never be thirsty again, nor will I have to come
here to draw water."*

*"Go and call your husband," Jesus told her, "and
come back."*

"I don't have a husband," she answered.

*Jesus replied, "You are right when you say you
don't have a husband. You have been married to five
men, and the man you live with now is not really your
husband. You have told me the truth."*

*"I see you are a prophet, sir," the woman said. "My
Samaritan ancestors worshipped God on this mountain, but you Jews say that Jerusalem is the place
where we should worship God."*

*Jesus said to her, "Believe me, woman, the time will
come when people will not worship the Father either on
this mountain or in Jerusalem. You Samaritans do not
really know whom you worship; but we Jews know whom
we worship, because it is from the Jews that salvation
comes. But the time is coming and is already here, when
by the power of God's spirit people will worship the Father as he really is, offering him the true worship that
he wants. God is Spirit, and only by the power of his
Spirit can people worship him as he really is."*

*The woman said to him, "I know that the Mes-
siah will come, and when he comes, he will tell us
everything."*

*Jesus answered, "I am he, I who am talking with
you."*

*At that moment Jesus' disciples returned, and they
were greatly surprised to find him talking with a*

woman. But none of them said to her, "What do you want?" or asked him, "Why are you talking with her?"

Then the woman left her water jar, went back to the town, and said to the people there, "Come and see the man who told me everything I have ever done. Could he be the Messiah?" So they left the town and went to Jesus.

In the meantime, the disciples were begging Jesus, "Teacher, have something to eat!"

But he answered, "I have food to eat that you know nothing about."

So the disciples started asking among themselves, "Could somebody have brought him food?"

"My food," Jesus said to them, "is to obey the will of the one who sent me and to finish the work he gave me to do. You have a saying, 'Four more months and then the harvest.' But I tell you, take a good look at the fields; the crops are now ripe and ready to be harvested! The man who reaps the harvest is being paid and gathers the crops for eternal life; so the man who plants and the man who reaps will be glad together. For the saying is true, 'One man plants, another man reaps.' I have sent you to reap a harvest in a field where you did not work; others worked there, and you profit from their work."

Many of the Samaritans in that town believed in Jesus because the woman had said, "He told me everything I have ever done." So when the Samaritans came to him, they begged him to stay with them, and Jesus stayed there two days.

Many more believed because of his message, and they told the woman, "We believe now, not because of what you said, but because we ourselves have heard him, and we know that he really is the Savior of the world."

JOHN 4:5–42

St. John strongly endorses the universalism of Isaiah in the story of the Samaritan woman at the well. Jesus converses with a woman (who because she comes to the well by herself and not with the other women may not be all that virtuous) who moreover is a Samaritan, worse than a heretic in the Jewish view of things, thus breaking two taboos. Small wonder that the apostles are astonished when they returned to the well and found Jesus and the woman talking. Like much of St. John's Gospel the story is a mixture of deft and fascinating details, brisk dialogue, and mystical reflection.

Jesus turns his full charm on the woman when he asks for a drink. This is simply not done, especially between Jews and Samaritans. Jesus quickly sweeps away this distinction. The conversation is between two human beings by a historic old well at the foot of a mountain. The woman does not want to talk about religion, she tries to evade his probing questions and keep the conversation on the safe issue of the differences between Jews and Samaritans. Jesus will not be distracted by a debate about the proper place to worship God. The Father-in-Heaven wants those who worship in spirit and truth—which does not mean they have no place to worship but that the issue is not place but who is the God that is worshiped. The Father-in-Heaven is not bound to any place, any language, any culture, any gender. He is rather a God for everyone and every place. One can imagine the woman's confusion. The man to whom she presumably has given a drink of water is charming, clever, sees right through her, and does not condemn her, but treats her with respect. In fact, he seems to find her amusing. It seems that he wants her, but not sexually, a want she understands all too well. Then he bluntly claims to be the expected Messiah. At this point she is dazzled, overwhelmed, dizzy from the heat of the noonday sun and from the strange appeal of this good and wise man who knows her all too well but still smiles gently, even laughs at her. It has been a long time that someone has treated her as a human person and ignored her sordid record. She must run off to collect her friends from the town, tell them about her newfound friend, and drag them off to the well to listen to him.

The apostles arrive at the scene, try to hide their all too obvious dismay that Jesus is conversing with a woman, a Samaritan woman, and a Samaritan woman who is not accepted by her own people. Here St. John inserts a discourse on the harvest, which is appropriate as an explanation for the conversation. The apostles still don't understand. Why does the Master have to do strange and bizarre things so often? It is disconcerting. They are just a little tired of his surprises. The woman, on the other hand, is transformed by her experience of the surprising Jesus. Probably an outcast in the town, she is not afraid to spread the news about the extraordinary man she met at the well and to

convince many of the people in the town to come out and
meet him. They follow her in spite of themselves because
the enthusiasm of this suddenly transformed woman is
contagious.

I have stressed the physical appeal of Jesus in his interac-
tion with women. Because he represented the Father-in-
Heaven, an incredibly charming God, Jesus had to be the
most charming man who ever lived. His eyes, his expres-
sions, his smiles, his posture, his laughter, must have melted
human hearts, male and female. He attracted people because he was attractive, he won them because he was win-
ning, he excited them with his good news because the good
news so animated him. Despite some Christian art and
piety, Jesus was not a creep, not a grim, dour prophet of
gloom. He could become angry and utter furious denuncia-
tions (though he never denounced women or a woman).
But large crowds do not follow a somber, dull, melancholy
man with angry eyes and a thin rigid smile.

As a bearer of grace, a fountain of grace, Jesus was a
graceful man. He embodied good news, good news that he
preached indeed, but also that he radiated with the timber
of his voice, the quickness of his smile, the warmth of his
laughter, the twinkle in his eyes.

The Evangelists don't describe these characteristics because that was not the way people wrote in those days. Yet
we must conclude that he was this kind of person because
of the way women and men reacted to him.

Consider the emotions of the Samaritan woman that
must have rushed through her soul from the beginning of
her encounter with Jesus. Attraction, suspicion, fear, a

sense of spiritual nakedness as he peeled away the protective layers in her soul, joy at the liberation he promised, doubt that he was the One Who Was to Come, and then finally liberating faith in the good news of the kingdom of God. Only one person is Jesus' harvest that day, but one totally transformed person, captivated for the rest of her life by the good news.

Only when he was dealing with hypocrites did Jesus lose his temper. With ordinary people who had ordinary faults and ordinary fears he won them over by his sympathy, his respect, and, above all, his charm. The Father-in-Heaven, the God of Isaiah, the creator of the world, had filled creation with his charm. He was not a God who would be bound to Mount Zion or Mount Gerizim or any of the other mountains. Rather he filled the world with his exuberant goodness and his only son would reveal by his body and his word the same exuberance.

As I write these words I find myself wondering why this graceful exuberance of Jesus has almost disappeared in the Christian traditions. Everywhere we turn in the Gospels we see it, but rarely in our homilies and sermons and catechisms. Moreover, everywhere we turn in the Gospels we find his delight in and respect for women, yet awareness of this delight is all too rare in the daily life of the Churches, including my own.

When I speak of graceful exuberance and of irresistible charm am I saying that Jesus was a charismatic leader? I'm saying more than that: Jesus defines charisma because he reflects, indeed embodies, the overwhelming energy of the grace of the charismatic Father-in-Heaven. The trouble with the word charisma is that these days it often implies a weakness, a propensity to use powerful appeal to manipulate others. Consider, however, the nature of Jesus' charisma in the story. The woman finds him very appealing because of course he is very appealing, but also a little frightening because he is a Jew, because he is a stranger, and because she is alone with him and defenseless. Then she is intrigued by his words but tries to fend him off with ethnic debate. He sees through her and she is then truly defenseless and wants to run to cover herself. Then his gentle strength reassures her and she knows she has met salvation and runs to town to share the good news with those who were once her enemies.

As John Shea says in his commentary on the next story, "Gentle, steady strength is a key characteristic in the Gospel portrait of Jesus." His strength comes from his consciousness of being loved by God and being the bearer of the holy Spirit into a world of suffering and alienation. This consciousness is constant. It permeates all he says and does. So many situations and so many voices try to pull him away from this inner truth. . . . But he holds fast to his vision. Jesus' charisma is a combination of exuberant grace and slow, steady gentleness.

❧ A Gentile Woman ❧

Then Jesus left and went away to the territory near the city of Tyre. He went into a house and did not want anyone to know he was there, but he could not stay hidden. A woman, whose daughter had an evil

*spirit in her, heard about Jesus and came to him at
once and fell at his feet. The woman was a Gentile,
born in the region of Phoenicia in Syria. She begged
Jesus to drive the demon out of her daughter. But Jesus answered, "Let us first feed the children. It isn't
right to take the children's food and throw it to the
dogs."*

*"Sir," she answered, "even the dogs under the table
eat the children's leftovers!"*

*So Jesus said to her, "Because of that answer, go
back home, where you will find that the demon has
gone out of your daughter!"*

*She went home and found her child lying on the
bed; the demon had indeed gone out of her.*

MARK 7:24–30

In this story from Mark's Gospel, Jesus meets a woman
who is doubly unclean, a gentile and the mother of a deeply
troubled daughter. Jesus has preached that the kingdom of
God is for everyone, but he has so far avoided gentiles,
probably because he felt he had to prepare his followers before they ventured into the world beyond Judaism. Some
critics think that this is a story that the early Christians
added to the Gospel to justify their decision to begin their
mission to the gentiles. However, Sean Freyne argues that
it is consistent with Jesus' vision of a kingdom of the
Father-in-Heaven in which such distinctions would disap-
pear. As a Galilean Jesus could not ignore the gentiles who
lived among the Galileans and all around them.

If there is a single characteristic that marks all of Jesus' relationships with women, it is his unfailing courtesy. Presumably his good mother had raised him to be always polite with women. Even though his words in the dialogue with her may have sounded harsh, we must assume that he was both courteous and attentive. She was vulnerable, defenseless, in desperate need of his help. She also sensed that this strong and gentle man admired her courage and that he would help her. We know from the parables to which we to turn in the next chapter that, in Robert Funk's words, it was to those who are utterly weak that the mercy of the kingdom most readily comes. Of course we are all in the final analysis utterly weak, mere bits of cosmic flotsam existing between two poles of nothingness. Jesus sees the woman's trust and faith, admires her greatly, and knows full well what he is going to do.

As John Shea writes, "What really intrigues me is his endless quest to give this steady strength. He thinks nothing of crossing the boundaries of Jew and gentile, and man and woman, to find the resonating response he so desires. Wherever he is positively received, he stays. When he is rejected, he moves on. And he follows clues. If one gentile can open completely to God, he will travel a great way to find others."

So Jesus surprised this pagan woman because of her faith, not her faith in him, save as someone who could help. Nor her faith in her Phoenician gods. But faith in the ultimate goodness she saw in Jesus, hence her faith of which she was not yet fully conscious.

She must have been frightened when she first approached this strange man, a foreigner, a Jew, a man who would probably look on her as hardly worth more than an insect. But she needed help. Her daughter was desperately ill. There was no one else to whom she could turn.

She must have sensed that this polite, somewhat aloof, but gentle and confident man not only could help her but would. Somehow her confidence resonated with his. She went through the difficult dialogue with him, understanding that they were playing a little game and knowing, deep down, she would win. She could sense his regard for her in the tilt of his head and the glow in his eyes. He not only respected her, he admired her for her courage. His final words were a surprise—in Jesus' stories there is always surprise—she was overjoyed with her victory in their word game, but also understood that there had never been any doubt. She would never forget him. Doubtless she would tell her grandchildren the marvelous story of the kind and gentle but very strong Jewish man who had cured their mother. It was, she would say, the most wonderful surprise of her life.

❧ *A Sinful Woman* ❧

A Pharisee invited Jesus to have dinner with him, and Jesus went to his house and sat down to eat. In that town was a woman who lived a sinful life. She heard that Jesus was eating in the Pharisee's house, so she brought an alabaster jar full of perfume and stood behind Jesus, by his feet, crying and wetting his feet with her tears. Then she dried his feet with her hair, kissed them, and poured the perfume on them.

When the Pharisee saw this, he said to himself, "If this man really were a prophet, he would know who this woman is who is touching him; he would know what kind of sinful life she lives!"

Jesus spoke up and said to him, "Simon, I have something to tell you."

"Yes, Teacher," he said. "Tell me."

"There were two men who owed money to a money-lender," Jesus began. "One owed him five thousand silver coins, and the other one fifty. Neither of them could pay him back, so he canceled the debts of both. Which one, then, will love him more?"

Simon said in reply, "The one, I suppose, whose larger debt was forgiven."

He said to him. "You have judged rightly."

Then he turned to the woman and said to Simon, "Do you see this woman? When I entered your house, you did not give me water for my feet, but she has bathed them with her tears and wiped them with her hair. You did not give me a kiss but she has not ceased kissing my feet. You did not anoint my head but she has anointed my feet with her ointment. So I tell you her many sins have been forgiven, hence she has shown great love. But the one to whom little is forgiven loves little."

He said to the woman, "Your sins are forgiven . . . your faith has saved you. Go in peace."

LUKE 7:36–41

The medieval Church merged this story with that of Mary of Magdala and Mary of Bethany. It is true that the third Mary did anoint Jesus the day before Palm Sunday despite mutterings among those around the table about the waste. However, Mary of Bethany was little more than a child and hardly a great sinner. To our knowledge neither was Mary of Magdala, regardless of whatever emotional problems she might have had. It is surely possible that in the early oral and written traditions the various anointings may have become confused. Nonetheless, there is no reason to combine them save perhaps to simplify stories. Since there is a different surprise in each of the stories, it is better to keep them separate.

As we reflect on this story, we enter a cultural world that is distant from ours and difficult to understand—strange, exotic, a little weird. We know that instead of sitting on chairs around a table—the neat and sensible custom of the Teutonic tribes that we follow, the diners were reclining on couches around a table, a difficult and messy way to eat, one should think. And the washing and anointing of feet, that doesn't seem very sensible either, except when we realize that feet would be covered with dust and dirt (or mud) if the guest walked down a road instead of being carried by bearers—which is hard to imagine Jesus doing. Moreover, it is not our custom to permit people to stand around watching those who are eating their dinner, nor to permit strangers to kneel and clean and perfume the feet of a guest, a slave's work—or, if the guest is someone special, the host's work.

And who was this woman? Why was she there? Why was

she acting as a slave to Jesus? If we should be watching, courtesy of some sort of time machine, we would find her behavior sensual, exhibitionist, erotic, and probably in poor taste. We would wish that Jesus would wave her off, send her away, tell her that this was neither the time nor the place. We would notice as Jesus did the whispered complaints and wonder why he didn't see that they might have a point. Why was he permitting a well-known courtesan to slobber all over him?

Candidly, this was behavior perhaps acceptable in a spa, maybe a Japanese spa, but why was the embodied second person of the Blessed Trinity tolerating such excessive affection?

And what was going on in her mind? Did she think Jesus was some kind of god? Well, maybe he was, but that sort of Christology had yet to emerge. She was a sinner, certainly, indeed a public sinner. All right, but why come to Jesus to admit her sins in what was a highly questionable public spectacle? Had she confessed her sins to him previously? Had she been moved by his vision of an implacably forgiving God? Had she realized that it was possible to change her life and start all over again? Or had she fallen in love with Jesus as a source of forgiveness and new beginnings? Or all of the above?

We simply don't know. The Gospel writer doesn't tell us, perhaps because he doesn't know. He has encountered the story in the traditions that he had inherited. It was a memory that the early Church treasured, perhaps because they liked to see Jesus putting down the hypocritical Pharisee. It was not important to them who the woman was or why she was there. She was a sinner who was doing penance and receiving forgiveness. Jesus surprised Simon with his put-down and surprised her with his forgiveness. That was enough to satisfy them. Did the early Christians raise an eyebrow or two at Jesus' tolerance for such an erotic display? Should one assume that they did not or the story would not have persisted in the tradition? Or were they as puzzled as we are?

The question they probably did not ask but we certainly do ask is how Jesus felt as she was washing and anointing his feet, making herself a virtual slave to him and exposing her total vulnerability for all to see? Did he enjoy the emotional abandon of her sobs and tears, something definitely not part of the ordinary feet-washing ritual?

I don't see how we can say that he did not. If he were utterly unmoved by it, he would not have been human. It was something she needed to do and he tolerated that. Presumably he did not want it as a daily occurrence. He surely knew when and how to indicate gently that enough was enough, that her self-humiliation had gone far enough and it was time to stop. I wouldn't be surprised that she knew too. Erotic tension? Surely. Emotions gone over the top? Everyone who knew Jesus knew that he would not permit that. Perhaps that is the reason the early Christians were not afraid of the story, at least not too afraid of it.

Why did the reformed sinner take such a terrible chance? She risked total vulnerability by invading that dinner and throwing herself at the feet of Jesus. Perhaps she provides a clue to one of the characteristics of Jesus that she shared with all the other women in his life. She knew that she was safe with him, that she had nothing to fear from him or from anyone else in the room. Women knew intuitively that Jesus would protect them.

In any event Jesus, with his usual gentle strength, protected her from the naysayers around the dinner and sent her forth a forgiven sinner, a renewed person with a fresh beginning for her life.

Can't beat that as a surprise.

✸ *A Father's Daughter* ✸

Jesus went back across to the other side of the lake. There at the lakeside a large crowd gathered around him. Jairus, an official of the local synagogue, arrived, and when he saw Jesus, he threw himself down at his feet and begged him earnestly, "My little daughter is very sick. Please come and place your hands on her, so that she will get well and live!"

Then Jesus started off with him. So many people were going along with Jesus that they were crowding him from every side.

There was a woman who had suffered terribly from severe bleeding for twelve years, even though she had been treated by many doctors. She had spent all her money, but instead of getting better she got worse all the time. She had heard about Jesus, so she came in the crowd behind him, saying to herself, "If I just touch his clothes, I will get well."

She touched his cloak, and her bleeding stopped at

once; and she had the feeling inside herself that she was healed of her trouble. At once Jesus knew that power had gone out of him, so he turned around in the crowd and asked, "Who touched my clothes?"

His disciples answered, "You see how the people are crowding you; why do you ask who touched you?"

But Jesus kept looking around to see who had done it. The woman realized what had happened to her, so she came, trembling with fear, knelt at his feet, and told him the whole truth. Jesus said to her, "My daughter, your faith has made you well. Go in peace, and be healed of your trouble."

While Jesus was saying this, some messengers came from Jairus' house and told him, "Your daughter has died. Why bother the Teacher any longer?"

Jesus paid no attention to what they said, but told him, "Don't be afraid, only believe." Then he did not let anyone else go on with him except Peter and James and his brother John. They arrived at Jairus' house, where Jesus saw the confusion and heard all the loud crying and wailing. He went in and said to them, "Why all this confusion? Why are you crying? The child is not dead—she is only sleeping!"

They started making fun of him, so he put them all out, took the child's father and mother and his three disciples, and went into the room where the child was lying. He took her by the hand and said to her, "Talitha, koum," which means, "Little girl, I tell you to get up!"

She got up at once and started walking around.

(She was twelve years old.) When this happened, they were completely amazed. But Jesus gave them strict orders not to tell anyone, and he said, "Give her something to eat."

MARK 5:21–44

St. Mark, master writer that he is, rarely permits a distraction in his stories that heightens the suspense. But the synagogue leader's plea for his dying daughter and Jesus' prompt response that he would visit her is temporarily sidetracked by the incident of the woman with a constant flow of menstrual blood, a condition that made her permanently impure according to the Jewish ritual laws. No matter how much time she spent in the ritual baths (for which the water jars at the marriage in Cana were doubtless intended), her blood kept flowing. For twelve long years she had suffered this humiliation and had wasted her resources on doctors. She knew that Jesus worked wonders so she followed him in the crowd that surrounded him, hoping a touch of his garment would heal her. Did Jesus know what was about to happen? Or, for a change, was he surprised too? What was this power inside him that could quickly affect cures? God's power, we say almost automatically. But it was not the limitless power of the creator, but a special gift the human Jesus possessed that we cannot name or understand. Jesus did wonderful things. He was critical of those who followed him seeking "signs and wonders." They wanted immediate magic and not the good news of the kingdom of God. His deeds were merely signs of the presence of the kingdom. But, we wonder, what was the faith about which he spoke so often at the time of a cure—the daughter of the Phoenician woman, the woman who bathed his feet, this deeply troubled and now embarrassed woman who had "stolen" some of his power.

Faith in the Father-in-Heaven about whom Jesus had spoken so often? Faith in Jesus himself? Faith that Jesus was God? Faith in the God she had learned about from her own religious tradition? All those answers presume a theological sophistication that would be too much to demand.

I suspect that their "faith" was an openness to goodness in the world. Precisely because they were not hard, cynical pessimists, Jesus would work with them. They were the kind of people for whom he was especially alert as John Shea said in an earlier paragraph. They believed an ultimate reality was gracious and a world full of grace and recognized grace in Jesus. Surely that attitude represented an inclination to know the Father-in-Heaven about whom Jesus had come into the world to reveal.

With the poor woman, humiliated by her ritual impurity and embarrassed by her apparent theft of Jesus' power, he was his usual kind, gentle, and respectful self, as perhaps she anticipated he would be despite her fears. Jesus knew she could "hijack" his power only because she was already open to it. Hence quite literally her faith had cured her. Her disposition to grace made it possible for Jesus' healing grace to pour into her.

After this incident the story turns again to the daughter of Jairus. The poor man is told that his daughter is already dead. Why did Jesus, who on other occasions healed someone who was not present, not heal the little girl immediately?

Why not work the same quick cure as he had done for the daughter of the Phoenician woman? Why did he have to see her personally? Why did he pause to speak to the woman with a menstrual problem that he had already cured? Didn't he know how sick the little girl was? Moreover, he tells the crowd that she was not dead, only sleeping, the exact opposite of what he would say about Lazarus. Then inside the house, he told the pale, motionless child to arise, and sure enough, she did just that. Jesus, doubtless pleased with one more surprise, told the parents to give her something to eat because such a vigorous little child was doubtless hungry, a nice final touch. Two graceful surprises in one afternoon, not a bad day's work.

Was there any miracle in the incidents? We don't know enough of the details to judge. Jesus at any rate claimed only that he had awakened her. The parents must have been convinced it was a miracle. The little girl would hear many times in the years to come how the rabbi from Galilee had brought her back to life. A miracle or a wonderful surprise? The former perhaps, the latter certainly.

❧ *A Widow's Son* ❧

Jesus went to a town named Naim, accompanied by his disciples and a large crowd. Just as he arrived at the gate of the town, a funeral procession was coming out. The dead man was the only son of a woman who was a widow, and a large crowd from the town was with her. When the Lord saw her, his heart was filled with pity

*for her, and he said to her, "Don't cry." Then he walked
over and touched the coffin, and the men carrying it
stopped. Jesus said, "Young man! Get up, I tell you!"
The dead man sat up and began to talk, and Jesus gave
him back to his mother.*

LUKE 7:11–17

The miracle at Naim seems almost gratuitous. No one
asked Jesus for help. He saw a woman overwhelmed with
grief. Her husband was dead, she had now lost her son.
How many other women in Galilee were suffering similar
grief that day? That week? That year? Was it fair that this
particular woman be selected for a miracle? How many
grieving mothers have read this Gospel passage down
through the centuries and wondered why God has not performed a similar miracle for them? Jesus surely knew that
the son, even should he live fifty more years, would eventually die and that the mother herself would die too. He
was only postponing death for a little while. They would
both rise from the dead eventually anyway, would they
not? Why bother?

Such questions fail to take into account the intensity of
Jesus' compassion and the depth of his hatred of death. He
knew he would die, probably very soon. In the widow he
saw an image of his own mother. This suffering was intol-
erable. He could ease the pain and on the spur of the moment, so to speak, he did—without even being asked. The
implication of his spontaneous sympathy for the widow of
Naim seems to be that the Father-in-Heaven hates death

too and that he sent Jesus into the world to reveal that hatred. Again God weeps when the little baby cries.

Later Christian folklore dreamed that the daughter of Jairus and the son of the widow would become lovers. A pious tale perhaps and not to be taken seriously. However, in the atmosphere of surprises in which we are walking in these stories, almost anything becomes possible.

✤ Twelve Stories ✤

In these twelve stories of Jesus' attitudes and behavior toward women, we encounter a seamless tapestry. Told at different times and different places about different women and handed down in different traditions and presented to us in different Gospels, each with their own viewpoint, they all portray a consistent portrait of his relationship with women, a portrait that is both priceless for the Christian heritage and even today generally ignored.

Nowhere in the New Testament does Jesus denounce women, nowhere does he patronize them, nowhere does he condemn them. The story of his surprise at Naim shows how keenly he sensed their emotions. When they were sad he wanted to see them smile. When they were embarrassed, he wanted to see them regain their self-confidence. When they were sorry for their sins, he wanted to immediately reassure them.

One is unwise to underestimate Jesus' delight in surprises. Shea remarks that the best preparation for the death that will come to all of us is to develop a healthy capacity for surprise. For Jairus and the widow of Naim the message is clear: here is a big surprise for you. There are even more spectacular surprises ahead. Eye has not seen, nor has ear heard, nor has it entered into the mind that which the Father-in-Heaven has prepared for those who love him.

Jesus was the kind of man that women almost immediately find attractive—strong, vigorous, confident, intense, charming, but at the same time gentle, sensitive, sympathetic. He respected them and talked to them as equals. They were his companions on his travels, equals to the apostles. He liked them, understood them, indeed saw through them. In his presence they became transparent, unprotected, yet completely safe. He listened to them respectfully, enjoyed them, smiled at them, laughed tenderly at them, and delighted in their admiration. For women Jesus was a constant surprise. Why, they must have asked themselves, don't other men treat us the way he does?

Small wonder that they fell in love with him. Small wonder he responded with amused affection. Small wonder that they followed him to the cross, while their male colleagues were running away. Small wonder that they went to the tomb early in the morning the first day of the week. Finally small wonder that they were the heralds of his resurrection.

That is the way it must be in the kingdom of God, the rule of the Father-in-Heaven. The artificial barriers that separate different groups of humans must be swept away. Men are still men, women are still women, but they are, as St. Paul said, all one in Christ Jesus.

That is the way the early Christians remembered him in

the stories they told about him and the evangelists wrote in the Gospels—even though they perhaps had difficulty understanding them and may have been shocked. (The "Rabboni" scene in the garden outside of the tomb must have been especially difficult.) Even St. Paul, who had some understanding about how all humans are one in Christ Jesus and wrote respectfully to his women followers, nevertheless gave women demeaning and patronizing advice.

Some might be tempted to use the words of the current Governor of California. Jesus was a "girlie-man" who liked women, but could not hold his own in the rough and tumble competition of real men. He was not tough and aggressive like a real man should be. However, one need only to consider his competitiveness in the rough and tumble word games that rabbinic discourse demanded. He was as tough as he had to be in repelling the verbal sallies of his enemies. For a dazzling put-down no one will ever match "render to Caesar what is Caesar's and to God what is God's."

Real men can treat both women and other men as equals.

Some writers see evidence of a struggle of women for equality in the second and third century as reflected in the later Gnostic gospels. Such a claim seems dubious, not so much in principle but because of lack of data. Curiously the relationships between Jesus and women might have been written in our time because they represent a conscious ideal for which some women and men strive for today. Such people may be primitive Christians because they are among the first to fully comprehend that the stories about Jesus and women in the Gospels are not passing incidents peripheral to the main story but central to Jesus' vision of the kingdom of God. Nor are they beautiful but unattainable ideals. They are rather essential to his manifestation of what the Father-in-Heaven demands of those who have become members of the kingdom of God.

If one wants to know the quality of a man, one must study the way he treats women. Jesus is the model for all male followers of Jesus. One has to say that for much of the history of his followers that model has not been followed, not even seriously considered as a model. In the first century, even century and a half, after Jesus returned to the Father-in-Heaven, women seemed to have had some equality in the Church. After that, as Christianity gradually became more Romanized, attitudes toward women in the church drifted farther away from the model of Jesus. As the Church converted the Teutonic and Slavic tribes that replaced Rome, the model became even fainter. The Celts whose culture recognized the rights of women were in some times and places a little more likely to practice some kinds of equality. (Irish women always had the right to choose their own husbands.) The neglect of Jesus' relationships to women—and its essential demand as the will of the Father-in-Heaven—was codified by St. Augustine who, for all his brilliance as a theologian, was one of the great cads of human history. Medieval teachers, utterly oblivious to the model of Jesus, referred to women as swamps that devoured men and glittering tombs filled with dead men's bones. The seminary I attended was committed to the necessity of avoiding women at all costs—a long, long way from the women who followed Jesus in the apostolic band. Some of the worst "male chauvinism" today exists among the clergies of the various churches and, alas, even worse among the hierarchies. Bible Christians, committed as they are to minute attention to the text of Scripture, don't seem to notice the example of Jesus. Such groups as the Promise Keepers seem incapable of shrugging off their views of male superiority.

And this is the green wood. In most areas of the world, women are in the same condition of near chattel slavery in which they have always existed since our species came down out of the trees. As I write these words, the Iraqi parliament is busy amending its constitution to restore the rule of religious law for women that existed before Saddam Hussein. The kingdom of heaven may be near, but it still has a long way to go. Followers of Jesus do not yet get the vision of Isaiah for which Jesus lived and died.

As in so many other areas (slavery, freedom, democracy) the leaven of the kingdom has contributed to the gradual changes, but with little help from the Churches that claim to speak for the kingdom. I admit that Christianity still teaches the way of Jesus, still tells his stories, still celebrates his vision, but often with little attention to what it should mean for the inner structures of the Churches. In my own tradition for a long time women (so long as they were nuns) had more check-signing power than in any other large corporation, but even that distinction has been lost.

I have never heard a sermon (homily these days) about the example of Jesus as a model for male behavior toward women. I suspect most preachers still don't get it—and many will denounce me for the "radical feminism" of this essay. As they say in New York, what can I tell ya!

Many men who claim to be followers of Jesus are still insensitive brutes who see no need to change nor even to examine their consciences. There is surely an impulse in the male of the species to treat women with reverence and respect and act as though they are equal humans and some manage to follow that impulse more or less. Yet the macho masculinity of the locker room remains pervasive.

If Jesus says to me that the kingdom of God is at hand or even that it's among us, I will take his word for it. But I will reply that often it is just barely visible even among his followers and that it has a long way to go. It may be just a foot above the head of the woman from Kerry, but there's a lot of fog in between.

The "Great Parables"

Part of the genius of Jesus' parable-making is his ability to take everyday experiences, such as sowing and reaping, and weave these into narratives that are at one and the same time highly realistic in terms of his hearers' world and their experiences and deeply resonant of Yahweh's activity on behalf of Israel as this had been described in the Psalms and the Prophets. For his peasant hearers their everyday work and experiences were being elevated to a symbolic level in the Psalms with reference to God's caring presence to Israel, as also in the proverbial wisdom in the Hebrew Scriptures. The element of surprise and dislocation that many of these stories contain was intended to challenge the hearers to reconsider their understanding of God and his dealings with Israel, and to experience his presence in the world of the everyday, the world of home, village, field, sky and mountain. The parables of Jesus are such successful religious metaphors because they are the product of a religious imagination that is deeply grounded in the world of nature and the human struggle with it, and at the same time deeply rooted in the traditions of Israel which speak of God as creator of heaven and earth and all that is in them.

SEAN FREYNE
Jesus, a Jewish Galilean

I F WE HAD available only the four parables that I call "Great," we would know who the Father-in-Heaven is. They represent Jesus' experience of the Father. They tell us who the God was that sent his son Jesus into the world to reveal him to those with whom he shared humanity. The God of the Great Parables is the God of Jesus, the God whose kingdom began with Jesus and continues even today. The God who was embracing the world in his kingdom had to be a very large God and a very generous one—how large and how generous these four parables try to tell us. To anticipate my conclusion, the God of Jesus is a God so deeply in love with his creatures that if humans should behave the same way, they would be deemed crazy.

Any theology that questions this insight has no claim to be Christian.

I have changed the titles of three stories to emphasize the image of God Jesus intended. "The Workers in the Vineyard" becomes "The Crazy Vintner"; "The Prodigal Son" becomes "The Indulgent Father"; and "The Woman Taken in Adultery" becomes "The Lenient Judge." Only "The Good Samaritan," it seems to me, is properly titled.

A parable is a narrative metaphor, a story in which one reality is compared to another. Some scholars say that parable is the first component of communication between humans, anticipating and making necessary language. It is in the nature of parable that one and only one reality is compared to another. It is also necessary that the comparison grabs the attention of the one who hears it (or reads it) because it is simultaneously surprising and illuminating. Parable is indeed the language of paradox and surprise. To say God is like a vintner who goes out early in the morning to hire workers, for example, is a jarring comparison though if, on hearing the story, one reflects thoughtfully on it, it could become powerfully illuminating. One cannot really explain a parable, because the one who hears it either "gets it" (either on first hearing or reflection) or does not. If the storyteller is backed into a corner and asked to explain, he can try but the very fact that someone demands an explanation suggests that an openness to wonder and surprise is not present and an explanation won't do any good.

✺ Parable and Allegory ✺

"Once there was a man who went out to sow grain. As he scattered the seed in the field, some of it fell along the path, and the birds came and ate it up. Some of it fell on rocky ground, where there was little soil. The seeds soon sprouted, because the soil wasn't deep. But when the sun came up, it burned the young plants; and because the roots had not grown deep enough, the plants soon dried up. Some of the seed fell among thornbushes, which grew up and choked the plants. But some seeds fell in good soil, and the plants bore grain: some had one hundred grains, others sixty, and others thirty." And Jesus concluded, "Listen, then, if you have ears . . .

"Those who hear the message about the kingdom but do not understand it are like the seeds that fell

along the path. The Evil One comes and snatches away
what was sown in them. The seeds that fell on rocky
ground stand for those who receive the message gladly
as soon as they hear it. But it does not sink deep into
them, and they don't last long. So when trouble or per-
secution comes because of the message, they give up at
once. The seeds that fell among thornbushes stand for
those who hear the message; but the worries about this
life and the love for riches choke the message, and they
don't bear fruit. And the seeds sown in the good soil
stand for those who hear the message and understand
it; they bear fruit, some as much as one hundred, oth-
ers sixty, and others thirty."

MATT. 13:1–24

People want explanations. Why did you write that book?
Why did you tell that story?

Thus the various Gospel stories about the kingdom of
heaven being like a farmer planting in his field and the crop
producing a hundredfold despite all the obstacles—one of
the parables of reassurance—is a story of the ultimate tri-
umph of the plans of the Father-in-Heaven despite all the
resistance throughout the ages. The explanation of it in
Matthew's Gospel is an allegory that perverts the point of
the parable. It misses the main thrust of the metaphor and
compares the individual components of the story to various reactions to the news of the kingdom. The apostles are
depicted as asking for an explanation, which the Gospel
author provides. I doubt that Jesus ever explained a parable.
To have to do that is to have failed as a storyteller, either

because the storyteller has not done a good job or because the audience is deliberately resistant to parables. ("Hard of heart," Jesus might have said.) Allegory also deprives the story of its punch because such explanations, while sometimes clever, are also anticlimactic. Oh, says the listener, is that what it means? Why all the fuss? The mystery, the surprise, the puzzle, fade away. The storyteller thinks that maybe he'd better find another audience.*

The Great Parables are all about God, the Father-in-Heaven, and his kingdom. The vintner is God, the indulgent father is God, the Good Samaritan is God. These parables are about God—the God of the kingdom, the God Jesus discloses to us—and his relationship to his people. They are about a passionately, desperately, insanely forgiving God.

While allegories are a legitimate narrative form, they lack the punch, the bite, the surprise of the parable. The parable has one and only one point. When it is converted to an allegory, as some of them were in the very early traditions of the Church, the one point is diffused among many clever interpretations and destroyed.

This understanding is, alas, not common among either clergy or laity. One can hear on any given Sunday when they turn up in the readings a vast array of inept homilies that try to deal with the complexities of very simple stories by spinning off clever and allegoric interpretations.

---

* As a storyteller I know the experience of a story becoming an inkblot for the personal, religious, and ideological demons that afflict those who try to tell you what your story was about.

Complex sermons are often easier to create than simple ones. To be fair to the preachers, each of the Great Parables is set in a context in which either the redactor of the tradition or the evangelist himself may have missed the point. The story is told more or less the way Jesus told it but either the context does not make it clear what Jesus is about or a sentence at the end confuses the thrust of the story. For example, the Good Samaritan story—perhaps the Greatest of all of the Great Parables—is placed in a context of a rabbinic dialogue about who is the neighbor when in fact its thrust as a parable is that God is like the Good Samaritan, a far more powerful, not to say, disturbing metaphor. The proper conclusion is not "go and do in like manner," but that God's merciful love is excessive, too much altogether, intolerably frightening.

A Bible Christian would comment that since God is responsible for the word-for-word inerrancy of the Scripture, no mistake is possible in the arrangement of the text. In this view those scholars on whom I rely for my approach—from the German Lutheran Joachim Jeremias to the Jesus Seminar chairman Robert Funk*—do not understand how their careful analysis of a parable is not only unnecessary, but blasphemous. Obviously I disagree and believe that such rigid obsession with individual words and phrases comes close to idolatry. The Great Parables are not about labor-management relations, or child-rearing, or

---

* It was several years after my ordination and four years of seminary Scripture courses that I learned from Jeremias what parables were and what the parables were about.

neighborliness, or law enforcement. They are about God and nothing else but God. Indeed, they are about a Jewish God but the Jewish God filtered through the Isaiah element in the tradition. Understood that way, they are shocking, scandalous, and unbearably surprising. If God is really that way, well, then . . .

✸ The Crazy Vintner ✸

The kingdom of heaven is like this. Once there was a man who went out early in the morning to hire some men to work in his vineyard. He agreed to pay them the regular wage, a silver coin a day, and sent them to work in his vineyard. He went out again to the marketplace at nine o'clock and saw some men standing there doing nothing. So he told them, "You also go and work in the vineyard, and I will pay you a fair wage." So they went. Then at twelve o'clock and again at three o'clock he did the same thing. It was nearly five o'clock when he went to the marketplace and saw some other men still standing there. "Why are you wasting the whole day here doing nothing?" he asked them. "No one hired us," they answered. "Well then, you go and work in the vineyard," he told them.

When evening came, the owner told his foremen, "Call the workers and pay them their wages, starting with those who were hired last and ending with those who were hired first." The men who had begun to work at five o'clock were paid a silver coin each. So when the men who were the first to be hired came to be paid, they thought they would get more; but they too were given a silver coin each. They took their money and started grumbling against the employer. "These men who were hired last worked only one hour," they said, "while we put up with a whole day's work in the hot sun—yet you paid them the same as you paid us!" "Listen, friend," the owner answered one of them, "I have not cheated you. After all, you agreed to do a day's work for one silver coin."

MATT. 20:1–15

John Shea says that this is the most unpopular parable because people perceive it as being "not fair." Why did the loafers get paid for not working. It seems possible that Jesus was retelling a rabbinic story in which those who came at the eleventh hour worked so hard they earned a day's wage. Jesus' twist on the story must have shocked those who heard it for the first time, as much as it shocks us today.

I like to picture the vineyard owner as a very young man who had inherited his father's property and was running it for the first time. The neighbors must have thought him a soft-hearted young fool. His father had worked hard to build up the business and now the generous and impractical young man was frittering it away. Admittedly he went out very early in the morning to collect the available workers gathered together in the marketplace waiting for work. These men were day laborers whose family survival through the year depended on the work they did at critical times in the agricultural cycle. Those that were there at the earliest hour were likely to be the most ambitious and hardworking. The young owner showed wisdom and industry in arriving at the marketplace before any of his competitors could get there. Incidentally, the "shape-up" like that of the longshoremen in the classic film *On the Waterfront* was the labor market for day workers through most of human history, including for the immigrant workers that our own country exploits. It is tough on the old, the infirm, the feckless, the young, the lazy. The young owner avoided them by being in the marketplace early.

As Sean Freyne says in the quote previously, the Great Parables are stories told with rich detail drawn from the daily lives of those to whom Jesus first told them. Everyone knew how precious time was at harvesttime. The ripe wheat and the ripe grapes have to be snatched up quickly before a change in the weather would ruin the crops.

Moreover, his neighbors also could not but approve of his returning to the marketplace three more times. Even if the quality of the work would deteriorate with the time the men bothered to come to the marketplace, it was still a good decision at harvesttime to gather as many laborers as he could before someone else claimed them. This was a critical day in the harvest. The owner of the vineyard made what my economist colleagues would call a rational choice. The workers who were hanging around throughout the day were not as industrious, but he would not pay them less. Even if they might not pick as many grapes as the dawn crowd, they would still put grapes into baskets that otherwise would remain on the vines to be devastated by a deluge of rain or a bitter wind or a sandstorm. The young man knew how to use his capital resources.

It was the recruitment of the slackers who ambled into the marketplace at the end of the day that seemed quite strange to the neighbors. Given the importance of this time of the year for income to support their families, these laggards could not have been industrious workers. Either lazy or infirm, they were going through the motions without any serious expectation of employment. The owner of the vineyard, unless he was a complete idiot, would not expect many baskets of grapes from them. He had passed out of the realm of rational choice into the misty world of foolish idealism when he hired these men. He was thinking of the hungry winter days ahead for their families. That was generous of him, but it was a mistake to confuse generosity with sound business practice.

However, those who had listened to the story from the point of view of the owner's neighbors likely had heard the story many times before. They knew how it ended. The men of five in the afternoon suddenly experienced a transformation and, uncharacteristically, worked so hard that they earned the silver coin that was the day's wage. Perhaps they wondered what sort of "O. Henry" ending Jesus might end the story with (though of course they had never heard of O. Henry).

They were startled, shocked, disturbed by Jesus' twist. Instead of the pious moral of the original story he portrayed the five o'clock crowd as more interested in how much they'd be paid than in doing any work. They were slackers to the bitter end, preparing to argue with the owner of the vineyard that he was unjust to them. Such men deserved no more than a pittance.

The protagonist of Jesus' story, however, did a terrible thing. He paid everyone the same. Even the five o'clock slackers received the silver coin, much to the dismay of those who had worked the whole day.

The farmer was not only unjust, he was off-the-wall crazy. This is God?

The answer was, yes, this is God. The story was not about labor relations nor about economic justice nor about rational economic choice. It was about God, a God who was so expansive, abundant, and loving in his generosity that humans who behaved with similar generosity, people would think insane. By human standards, God is quite mad. The parable is no longer a story about the need for diligence and industry among workers. The parable is about a crazy God, the Father-in-Heaven who is, it seems, too reckless in his generosity, too excessive altogether in his bounty. If Jesus' version scandalizes us after two millennia, how bizarre it must have seemed to those who heard it for the first time. Yet Jesus believed and asked us to believe that the universalistic God of Isaiah has to be exorbitant in his abundance or he isn't God.

It is much easier to deal with the odd economics of the parable than to deal with the image of a mad and perhaps madcap God.

In this parable as in the other Great Parables and in many others, there is a cast of three persons (noted in detail by Robert Funk)—the God symbol, the powerless person (laggard workers), and the "third man" (with a nod to the Graham Greene/Carol Reed film). The third man is the one who murmurs against God's generosity, either before the denouement of the story or immediately after. The dramatic tension, the buildup to Jesus' surprise, is almost a rabbinic dialogue, not surprising in a Jewish storyteller. Those of us who find the parable offensive today are in effect the third man. We want to argue over the economy of the story and not face the theological vision. The parable offers little comfort to those who, caught up in pre-counciliar Catholic theology, want to make comparisons between relative "places in heaven." Surely the latecomers, the people who make it into the kingdom at the last minute, will not have as great a place in heaven as those who are cradle Catholics, will they?

John Shea wisely remarks that the abundance of the kingdom of heaven is indivisible. Once one embraces the worldview of the kingdom (Isaiah as interpreted by Jesus) God's excessive abundance is nonfrangible. It can be no more and no less than a single silver coin—given to those who by human standards no longer deserve it.

⚜ *The Indulgent Father* ⚜

There was once a man who had two sons. The younger one said to him, "Father, give me my share of the property now." So the man divided his property between his two sons. After a few days the younger son sold his part of the property and left home with the money. He went to a country far away, where he

wasted his money in reckless living. He spent every-
thing he had. Then a severe famine spread over that
country, and he was left without a thing. So he went to
work for one of the citizens of that country, who sent
him out to his farm to take care of the pigs. He wished
he could fill himself with the bean pods the pigs ate,
but no one gave him anything to eat. At last he came to
his senses and said, "All my father's hired workers
have more than they can eat, and here I am about to
starve! I will get up and go to my father and say, 'Fa-
ther, I have sinned against God and against you. I am
no longer fit to be called your son; treat me as one of
your hired workers.'" So he got up and started back to
his father.

He was still a long way from home when his father
saw him; his heart was filled with pity, and he ran,
threw his arms around his son, and kissed him. "Fa-
ther," the son said, "I have sinned against God and
against you. I am no longer fit to be called your son."
But the father called to his servants. "Hurry!" he
said. "Bring the best robe and put it on him. Put a
ring on his finger and shoes on his feet. Then go and
get the prize calf and kill it, and let us celebrate with
a feast! For this son of mine was dead, but now he is
alive; he was lost, but now he has been found." And so
the feasting began.

In the meantime the older son was out in the field.
On his way back, when he came close to the house, he
heard the music and dancing. So he called one of the
servants and asked him, "What's going on?" "Your

*brother has come back home," the servant answered,
"and your father has killed the prize calf, because he
got him back safe and sound." The older brother was
so angry that he would not go into the house; so his father came out and begged him to come in. But he spoke
back to his father, "Look, all these years I have
worked for you like a slave, and I have never dis-
obeyed your orders. What have you given me? Not
even a goat for me to have a feast with my friends! But
this son of yours wasted all your property on prostitutes, and when he comes back home, you kill the prize
calf for him!" "My son," the father answered, "you
are always here with me, and everything I have is
yours. But we had to celebrate and be happy, because
your brother was dead, but now he is alive; he was
lost, but now he has been found."*

LUKE 15:11–32

As John Shea remarks, if anyone in this story is prodigal,
it's the father. He is a generous and loving man with two
sons who are losers, the one a wastrel, the other a rigid ac-
countant of grievances. He spoils the two boys rotten and
continues his excessive love even though they are miser-
ably ungrateful in return. Again there is the dramatic pat-
tern of the God person (the father), the helpless person—in
this case a passive-aggressive and scheming wretch (the
first son), and the third man (the second son). The dialogue between the God symbol and the third man (and
us insofar as our complaints are against God's behavior)
is part of the structure of the story. Indeed, Robert Funk in

his book on parables suggests that this tripartite form of the story is sufficient reason to believe that the tale is an authentic work of Jesus. It reveals to us a characteristic stylistic formula of Jesus. The conversation among the three characters is the essential structure of the story, but if the listener wants to be caught up in the metaphor of the story and go beyond rigid exegesis, he must realize that s/he is the third man and consider what kind of person the first man is. Otherwise the listener sinks into an inescapable swamp of prose.

I imagine the neighbors of the prodigal father as a background chorus like the neighbors of the crazy vineyard owner—or of Job. They see the father as an extremely good man, kind, generous, loving. However, the poor fellow has one tragic flaw, one damning weakness. He worships his two sons all out of proportion to the obvious fact that from early childhood they were losers. Perhaps if he established rules for their behavior, insisted on self-discipline, and moderated his generosity with a decent common sense, they might have amounted to something—not great men surely, not even truly good men, but at least acceptable heirs to his lands and fortune. Like the obnoxious friends of Job they buzzed around him with child-rearing proverbs. He would nod his head sadly and agree but then say something like "I love them both so much."

These three men whom Jesus had appropriated into his story were surely familiar figures in the Galilee of his time, the rich landowner and his two worthless sons. Too bad the two of them could not be combined into one decent human being. Indeed, some of those who heard the parable must have suspected they knew the real-life counterparts of the men in the story. (They didn't.) Once again Jesus made vivid use of the everyday experiences of those who listened to the story. Yes, they would say, we know those kinds of men very well. They are local stereotypes.

The first son was an arrogant and extravagant flake. Convinced that his father was a pushover, he demanded his inheritance. He was fed up with the narrow and dull life of a farmer. He wanted to leave it all behind and travel to a place where life was exciting. He did not want to wait the long years before his father died. He wanted to have fun before he would be too old to enjoy it. So he made an outrageous, indeed an unheard of, demand. Turn over my part of the inheritance now. The neighbors would have said that the father should have turned down the request with a warning to the son that there was no guarantee that he would ever inherit anything unless he shaped up and demonstrated some sense of responsibility. Incredibly, however, the father divided his properties and gave half of them to the young rapscallion. One can imagine the older son, careful cautious bean counter that he already was, shaking his head in dismay. However, he knew what kind of a man his father was and did not waste his time with an effort to warn him.

There was no point in the warning. The father knew what his son would do with the property and gave it to him anyway. The son promptly sold it, collected his money, and departed to begin what he thought would be a full and exciting life. When the neighbors protested his folly, the father's only reply was, "He's my son and I love him."

The second son may well have celebrated. In the absence of his brother, the remaining properties would become more profitable and there would be more money for him when his father died.

The profligate son wasted his money. He had a grand time for a while and then it was all gone. As he worked with the hogs out in the country, he had only fading memories of the parties, the drinking, the women. No one cared about him. All his friends had deserted him. The women he had victimized despised him. He would soon die of hunger.

Then he realized that he should do penance and return to his father? So we are told by preachers who do not understand the story. There is no sign of grief in his thinking or in his preparation of the little recitation for his father. He was concerned only about his own survival and eventual comfort. The words he planned to say to his father were empty and cynical, designed only to manipulate the father, a style at which he had become skillful during a lifetime of manipulation. His parent, he knew, was a weak and prodigal man, as far as his sons were concerned. He expected that the old man would fall for blatant hypocrisy just as he always had. Unfortunately this pious reading of the story has caused some preachers to insist that the son was sorry, wanted forgiveness, and returned to beg his father's pardon. Such a reading deprives the parable of all its force. It is essential to the story that the son continues to be a phony and a hypocrite and that the father continues to love him despite his hypocrisy. There is nothing in the story that provides any reason to think that the first son is truly sorry for having hurt his father.

Later the neighbors would wonder why the old man welcomed back a dishonest, worthless son and why he organized a party to celebrate his return. That's no way to deal with such a troublesome young man. Yes, the father should accept him but he should insist that his errant offspring honor some conditions to prove his sorrow and his purpose of amendment. Establishing rules of a contact was not something that this loving father could possibly do. He was capable only of joy on the return of a lost son.

Parents today would agree with the neighbors. If a child had caused them so much grief, he would have to work hard to regain their approval. Indulgence is no way to deal with a family problem. Before long, the son would demand more money, run away again, and return to his wastrel ways. Did not the poor old man understand?

Note that the father is outside the house and looks down the road. The story seems to imply that he was there often, perhaps sitting on a porch or under a shade tree, hoping against hope that his beloved son would appear in the distance. Then he sees his long-lost son and rushes down the road to embrace him. He cuts short the carefully rehearsed speech, embraces the young scoundrel, welcomes him home, and proclaims a feast.

The wastrel doubtless rejoices to himself. He has fooled the old man again. He is being treated like a prince. Why did he wait such a long time to exploit his weakness? Meanwhile the other son, the third man, comes in from the fields, hears the noise of the singing and dancing (truly a great feast!), and protests to his father. Why so much for him and nothing for me!

Perhaps the reason many readers want to believe that the first son is truly contrite is that they want to sympathize with the second son, whom they believe received a bad deal. If they had read the text more carefully, they would have understood just how indulgent the old man was and be more deeply offended by his behavior. Like the second son they would be angry at the father, only more angry. His behavior is not only indulgent, it is positively unfair.

"Unfair!" that is the battle cry of third men in the parables.

The father tries to soothe the second son, nothing is being taken from him, he will receive the whole inheritance and his father has always loved him, but the lost has returned and should not they celebrate!

Yes, the begrudgers say, have a quiet, modest celebration for the wastrel and then a big celebration for the loyal son, even if he is a bit of a prig. It is the only fair thing to do.

In fact, both sons are losers, the first because of his senseless greed and the second because of his narrow, rigid envy. But the father proclaims his love for both of them, regardless of how they have behaved. One suspects he is in for more trouble from the two of them.

However, as John Shea says of the workers in the vineyard, the superabundance of God's merciful love is indivisible. God loves each of us with a passionate forgiving love, whether we be second men or third men. His love is implacable and will not be shaken, no matter how thin our merit is, or how selfish or envious we are, or how little we understand his love, or how much we try to force his passion for us into narrow economic models.

We don't want to accept the image of God in these two stories because that would make life too easy, because we would not fear damnation, because we could not bargain with God—trade off our good behavior for his rewards—because his relentless love would force us to give up the protection of self-hatred and self-pity.

How does one escape that kind of God?

There are two issues that arise from Jesus' stories of God. The first is whether God is really that way, if indeed there is a God at all. Thus would those who do not believe in God and those who believe in a God who is eagerly waiting to vaporize us when the Rapture comes make common cause.

The second is whether the God of these two stories is the God of Jesus, the God who must be like the prodigal father and the crazy vintner to carry out the vision of Isaiah, the Father-in-Heaven who has sent Jesus to announce the kingdom of heaven. About this issue there can be no doubt at all. Both these madcap, extravagant men are symbols of the Father-in-Heaven.

Such an image of an indulgent, excessively loving God may be scary, offensive, scandalous. However, there can be no doubt that such is the Father-in-Heaven.

❧ *The Good Samaritan* ❧

A teacher of the Law came up and tried to trap Jesus. "Teacher," he asked, "what must I do to receive eternal life?"

*Jesus answered him. "What do the Scriptures say?
How do you interpret them?"*

The man answered, " 'Love the Lord your God
with all your heart, with all your soul, with all your
strength, and with all your mind'; and 'Love your
neighbor as you love yourself.' "

"You are right," Jesus replied; "do this and you
will live."

But the teacher of the Law wanted to justify himself, so he asked Jesus, "Who is my neighbor?"

Jesus answered, "There was once a man who was
going down from Jerusalem to Jericho when robbers
attacked him, stripped him, and beat him up, leaving
him half dead.

"It so happened that a priest was going down that
road; but when he saw the man, he walked on by on
the other side. In the same way a Levite also came
there, went over and looked at the man, and then
walked on by on the other side. But a Samaritan who
was traveling that way came upon the man, and when
he saw him, his heart was filled with pity. He went
over to him, poured oil and wine on his wounds and
bandaged them; then he put the man on his own ani-
mal and took him to an inn, where he took care of
him. The next day he took out two silver coins and
gave them to the innkeeper. 'Take care of him,' he told
the innkeeper, 'and when I come back this way, I will
pay you whatever else you spend on him.' "

And Jesus concluded, "In your opinion, which one

of these three acted like a neighbor toward the man
attacked by robbers?"
    The teacher of the Law answered, "The one who
was kind to him."
    Jesus replied, "You go, then, and do the same."

LUKE 10:25–37

The second man in the parables is always weak and helpless, the laggard worker and the starving if hypocritical older
son. However, this thesis that runs through all of the Jesus
stories is more obvious in the parables of the Good Samaritan
and of the woman taken in adultery. The wounded Jew and
the sinful woman are about to die.

Luke, in some respects the most cautious and careful of
the evangelists, seems to have missed the point in this story—
which demonstrates how easily even the most faithful of the
early Christians dodged the scandal of the parables. He
makes it a morality tale. It is a good morality tale, that's why
Luke inserted it into a dialogue about neighbors. However, it
almost certainly was not told that way by Jesus. As Robert
Funk puts it:

"All those who are truly victims, truly disinherited,
truly helpless, have no choice but to give themselves up to
mercy. And mercy comes from the quarter where it is least
expected. Grace is always a surprise. As a parable the story
of the Good Samaritan is a very powerful instrument. It
sets the message of Jesus in unequivocal terms for the audience. None could mistake it. It explains why IRS officials
and prostitutes understand the kingdom of heaven, whereas
theologians, Bible scholars, and professional pietists do not.

It explains why a hated alien must be the instrument of grace. It makes pretense on the part of the listener impossible. There is no other parable in the Jesus tradition which carries a comparable punch. The Christian community moralizes it in order to be able to live with it, and this is inverted testimony to its power."

I want to extend Funk's point. In the final analysis we are all, sociologists or drug lords, ultimately powerless in the face of God. We are all truly helpless. We cannot bargain with God, we cannot negotiate with him, we cannot make claims on him, we cannot force his hand. We are as dependent on his merciful love as the injured Jewish traveler was on the generous compassion of the Samaritan.

We don't really like that, though we have an absolute guarantee that God's love will envelop us, overwhelm us, smother us with compassion and concern as the Samaritan did the traveler. God will in effect stop at the inn to see how well we are recovering and pay our bill. Only when we are willing to put ourselves in a position of utter dependency on God will we understand the power, the surprise of his love. We are all wastrel sons and daughters, handicapped laborers, and men and women dying at the roadside. But the kingdom of heaven nonetheless closes in on us.

Making a Samaritan God would have been outrageous to the early Christians, even perhaps to a sensitive and sympathetic writer like St. Luke. Small wonder the story becomes a morality tale—and a useful one at that. My, isn't that a lovely story, we say. It tells us how we should behave to people we don't like and exposes the hypocrisy of the clergy. Isn't that wonderful!

But a generous foreigner, and a heretic at that, as a symbol of God! Wasn't Jesus really excessive in that story? Did he really expect to get away with something like that?

One can never say of storytellers what they expect to get away with. Yet Jesus must have known what he was doing. The Jew is the second man, the priest and the Levite are the third men, and the Samaritan was God.

Outrageous, scandalous, shameful, disgraceful—think of any word you might want to add and all might apply. This story of Jesus was all of these things. Yet it remained in the tradition because everyone knew Jesus had said it. St. Luke couldn't leave it out, but he tried to tame it. That a Samaritan could be a good guy was acceptable, if by way of exception, but that he might be a symbol for the Father-in-Heaven— how could he be that?

Any more than a Muslim or a Communist or an Atheist or a Radical Feminist or an Evangelical with a Bible under his arm or, to switch Professor Funk's word, an agnostic college professor . . . Could we see in their mercy a hint of God's mercy? No way.

A surprise surely, an unacceptable surprise.

But, Jesus is telling us, the Father-in-Heaven is unacceptably surprising, especially when we are totally weak, utterly defenseless, and completely at the Father-in-Heaven's mercy. As we will be at the moment of our death. We might even cry out for mercy, even if you are a Muslim or a Communist or an Atheist or a Bible-toting Evangelical!

Why in heaven's name, you should excuse the expression, would Jesus choose such outlandish metaphors? Would it not have been easier for the early Christians and perhaps for us today if a fellow Galilean Jew, perhaps even a woman—since he liked women so much—had taken care of the wounded traveler? Why did he have to beat us over the head with the darn Samaritan?

The answer surely must be, he wanted to make his point about the astonishment of God's mercy as strong as he possibly could. If a Samaritan could represent God's merciful love to a Jew, if an agnostic can represent that merciful love to a contemporary evangelical, then that mercy must be so powerful as to sweep all objections away. God's surprising love is indeed surprising beyond human capacity to comprehend.

✸ *The Lenient Judge* ✸

Then everyone went home, but Jesus went to the Mount of Olives. Early the next morning he went back to the Temple. All the people gathered around him, and he sat down and began to teach them. The teachers of the Law and the Pharisees brought in a woman who had been caught committing adultery. "In our Law Moses commanded that such a woman must be stoned to death. Now, what do you say?" They said this to trap Jesus, so that they could accuse him. But he bent over and wrote on the ground with his finger. As they stood there asking him questions, he straightened up and said to them, "Whichever one of you has committed no sin may throw the first stone at her." Then he bent over again and wrote on the ground. When they heard this, they all left, one by one, the older ones first. Jesus was left alone, with the woman still standing there. He straightened up and said to her, "Where are they? Is there no one left to condemn you?"

"No one, sir," she answered.

"Well then," Jesus said, "I do not condemn you either. Go, but do not sin again."

JOHN 8:1–11

The segment of St. John's Gospel in Chapter 8.1–11 has had a strange history. It must have circulated in some form in the later half of the first century and in the early part of the second century. The final author of the Fourth Gospel almost certainly included it in his version of the tradition. Yet some early codices of St. John do not contain it. Some writers think that it was excluded because it is so scandalous. Others suggest that it was a parable that was too "hot" to publish as such and became a story about Jesus somewhere in the developing tradition so that this shocking story would have the authority of Jesus behind it.

One may question how many women were stoned to death for adultery in the time of Jesus. However, Jewish law demanded it. Jesus recast the traditional teaching on divorce so that men could commit it as well as women. In Jewish law only a sinning woman was guilty of adultery against her husband. A man was guilty of adultery only against another man if he had copulated with the wife of the other man. Hence we perceive that Jesus would not be sympathetic to the stoning of a woman who had betrayed her husband.

The objections to this incredibly lenient treatment of a grave sin perhaps explains why in some Bibles today it does not appear or appears only in italics. I treat it as a parable because it has the classic parable form of the first man (the lenient judge), the second man (this time the woman), and the third man (the accusers). Moreover the woman is desperately in need of mercy—as such persons are in all the Great Parables.

We must be wary of the temptation of conflating women in Gospel stories in the interpretation of them. The woman is not Mary of Magdala or Mary of Bethany and it is most unlikely that she is the woman who anointed Jesus' feet at the home of Simon the Pharisee.

The judge indeed treats the woman with the same courtesy and respect that Jesus always displays when he's talking with women. That perhaps suggests that the story is not a parable but an actual event. However, I choose to depict it as a parable because it fits the form so neatly. Either way it is a story of God's superabundant mercy and love.

The judge is a very poor judge according to the tradition of Law under which he is supposedly operating—a tradition existing in many parts of the world until this day. A guilty woman must be put to death. A good judge would at least want to hear testimony, especially from her affronted husband. He might question the woman to see if she has anything to say in her own defense. The judge does not do either of these things. In fact, he doesn't seem to consider the matter seriously. He remains silent tracing designs in the dust. Perhaps he sympathizes with the woman and her fear and embarrassment.

He knows that the reason stoning is prescribed is not that the woman has been sexually immoral but that she has risked her husband's inheritance. His family's property might be lost to someone who is not of his seed.

Then he rises from the ground, stands up straight, and says, all right the one without sin should throw the first stone. Then he returns to his scribbling in the dust. One by one, the accusers drift away. Perhaps, as one of the Jesus films suggests, he was listing their sins.

The judge stands up again and looks around.

No more accusers, he says to the woman.

No one, she says.

Then neither will I condemn you. Sin no more.

Absolution without either contrition or a firm purpose of amendment!

It is difficult for us today to understand how intolerably lenient the judge was. Indeed he is insanely irresponsible. Adultery today is considered primarily a sin of sexual morality. She has betrayed the interpersonal bond between herself and her husband. In the days of Jesus a woman who commits it is stealing the property rights of her husband and his family, a horrendous violation of the social order. She must not only suffer a painful death because of her sin, she must be prevented from passing on those property rights to any child she might be carrying or endangering them once again with more adultery.

By dismissing these essential social norms as irrelevant, the judge threatens the stability of society. Good men, concerned about the family and its rights, might very well want to stone him. His conduct of the trial is slovenly, his

failure to consider evidence is irresponsible, his casual dis-
missal of the guilty woman is criminal.

Again the same refrain—God's justice is not our justice.
God's mercy far exceeds our mercy. If human judges were
as lenient as God is then they would be considered crimi-
nally insane.

✸ *Parables As Comedy* ✸

Dan Via, a scholar of the parables, says they are comedy.
Such an insight can suggest two important dimensions of
the parable as an art form. First, the Great Parables have
happy endings—for the vineyard workers, for the starving
son, for the Jewish traveler, and for the sinful woman.
Moreover they are comic in a second sense. The frustration
of the early-morning workers, of the second son, of the
priest and Levite, and of the accusers of the woman is
funny, almost slapstick. Jesus laughs at them and invites us
to laugh at them because they don't understand the length
and the width, the height and the depth of the implacably
forgiving love of God.

If you claim to be a follower of Jesus of Nazareth these
parables are terrible challenges and not only because you
find yourself often caught in the third man role. Once you
get beyond economic models of what is fair and are concerned about your "place in heaven," you must ask yourself
whether you really believe that God is the kind of God Jesus suggests, a God who is willing to forgive anyone who
gives the slightest hint of signing on for the kingdom of

heaven, a God who by the standards of human rulers is an easygoing buffoon, a God who expects you to model his forgiveness by forgiving others. A God who, for some god-forsaken reason, is crazy in love with you.

How wonderful and now embarrassing. Love like that makes demands as all great love does and those demands are insistent and persistent. The Father-in-Heaven is not a God to be trifled with.

Do you believe in such a God, a reader may demand of me, a God who can be symbolized by a crazy young farmer, a sinfully indulgent father, an excessively compassionate traveling heretic, and a judge lenient to the point of criminal insanity?

Moreover, the reader may demand to know whether I don't understand that to preach that kind of God may lead sinners to remain in sin till the end of their lives because God will forgive them anyway.

In response to the first question, yes, I believe in that God. Sometimes. As I write this meditation I realize how problematic my faith in the God of the parables really is. I certainly don't reject the parables of Jesus. On the contrary, I am convinced that they are the best news humankind has ever heard. Yet I tend to be a worrier. God understands that too, if Jesus is to be believed. He is aware of the fear that makes all of us worry. He is ready to tolerate that fear because he loves us so much. But . . . I continue to be afraid. Of death and of a lot of other foolish things.

Like how the third men will twist this meditation out of context and lie about it.

Yet the God in my stories and the God I preach with deep conviction is the God of the parables.

But do not the stories and the homilies about such a God incline people to take their chances at sin because they know God will forgive them at the last minute anyhow? Such an objection might better be proposed to Jesus who told his stories about the Father-in-Heaven he knew so well. Those rigid, conservative Catholics—clerical and lay—who don't want people to know what God is like seem to believe that it is necessary to keep them in the dark about God's mercy so that they will not sin. One must obfuscate the love of God so that people will fear him. They shouldn't be told about the workers of five in the afternoon or the hypocritical wastrel or the wounded Jew on the roadside or the adulterous woman.

This is a major divide among the followers of Jesus between those who take him at his word and those who are not willing to trust people with the good news. Make no mistake about it, the latter often seem to have a decisive advantage. We must force people to behave properly, they argue, or there will be a complete moral collapse. There is no effective way to respond to those who wish to impose a morality of fear as they play the role of Dostoyevsky's Grand Inquisitor. Fear of the Lord is not only the beginning of wisdom for them, it is the end.

One must simply say to them that they are wrong. They have separated themselves from Jesus of Nazareth who presumably knew more about human nature than they do. As I will say subsequently about the Parables of Urgency, Jesus warned his audiences of the dangers of taking the kingdom of God for granted. He insisted that we must take advantage of the kingdom of God while there is still time. When does a person's time end? That is not for us to say.

Is everyone saved? Do not at least some people suffer for all eternity pains in a hell that would make Dante's *Inferno* look like a parish carnival? The teaching of my own heritage on the matter is that one must believe that there is a hell, but one does not have to believe that anyone is in it. Thus we give God a free hand, which is generous of us, though God's hand is free even without our permission.

Origen, one of the great teachers of the early Church, believed in universal salvation. Two of the great theologians of the late twentieth century, Hans Urs Von Baltassar and Karl Rahner, the former more conservative, the latter more progressive, inclined in that direction. The late Pope John Paul II seemed sympathetic to such an idea, though he saw some problems in it.

I'm not qualified to say anything more than I hope so. Rahner argued that God's ingenuity was as powerful as his mercy. God simply does not give up.

Would Hitler find salvation? Cardinal George, in a sermon delivered at Bond Chapel in the University of Chicago, remarked that wouldn't it be an enormous achievement of God's mercy if he could accomplish the salvation of such a man. Some would not want God to try. Yet it is not up to us to question God's mercy and love.

There are other reasons that lead people to reject the Great Parables, while all the time professing to be Christian—envy and revenge.

Envy may be a more pernicious temptation than lust. Sexual desire can convert itself into love. Envy changes into even more envy. Desire is sated for at least a while. Envy is never satisfied. Desire sometimes seeks the happiness of its object, envy seeks the partner's destruction. Some humans are so deeply steeped in envy that it takes control of their lives.* They resent celebrities, people who are rich and successful, political leaders and their families, professional confreres, brothers and sisters, neighbors, children—anyone and everyone who seems to have more of anything and everything than they have.

The envious are descendants of the third man in the parables. They cannot abide that God's mercy would fall like the rain on the just and the unjust. They cannot tolerate that some celebrities be happy and then achieve salvation. The envious hate the universalism of the vision of Jesus and Isaiah. Because they are angry at most creatures, they are also angry at God for the unequal distribution of gifts and talents and success. Unless God does not spread talent evenly, they resent not only the talent but God himself.† Why am I not as beautiful as Julia Roberts, as sexy as Orlando Bloom. It's God's fault and it's not fair. The last rage of the envious person is that something is not "fair."

The deeply envious person experiences constant resentment. His life is twisted, contorted, wracked by resentment. There is no room in his soul for a generous God. Will such a person be saved? He will find it difficult, I think, to evade

---

* A Russian proverb describes envy perfectly. It says not that I wish I had my neighbor's cow, but I wish my neighbor's cow would die.
† An e-mail ranted at me because of a "chemical or biological accident" I was able to write and he wasn't.

the strategies and the tricks of an ingenious and passionately loving God.

A first cousin of envy is revenge. The envious person
wants revenge on the celebrities, even if it means stalking or
killing them. A person can find instant fame and glory by
killing a president. Not all vengeful persons are twisted by
envy, however. Rather, they want to "get even" for the bad
things others have done to them. In an ordinary life of ordinary length working at ordinary things one can compile
a long list of enemies and store up vast amounts of bad
memories. The personality then stores up oceans of sludge
that will be dumped on the enemies whenever it becomes
possible to do so. The bad memories will not go away, one
cannot wipe that segment of the brain clean. But one can
and should forgive, if only in one's heart.

Forgiveness is the problem with the God of Jesus, the
Father-in-Heaven. He forgives us, it would seem uncondi-
tionally. But there is a catch, as there often is with God. He
expects us to forgive others. The key phrase of the Lord's
Prayer is that we be forgiven as we forgive others. However, it is a misreading of the prayer to think that we earn
God's forgiveness by forgiving others. The bargain, if there
is one with a God who does not like bargains, is that we
forgive others *because* he has forgiven us. Our task is to
model, reflect, disclose the insanely forgiving God to others
who do not know him.

No grudges permitted.*

---

* We don't have to like the people we forgive, but we must relinquish the pleasure of plotting imaginary ways of getting even.

We forgive even those who have done us very great harm—taken away our job, ruined our career, stolen our money, butchered our spouse in a ghastly medical mistake, killed our children, raped us, abused us, tortured us. "Father forgive them, for they know not what they do."

Another girlie-man sentiment?

Those Christians of whatever denomination who rejoice in public at the end of a trial of someone who has done them grave harm and who say that "closure" will come only when the criminal is executed don't understand what it means to be a follower of Jesus or what closure involves psychologically.

I can't demand forgiveness from such folk, you say? I'm not demanding anything. I am merely suggesting that they have forgotten the words of the Lord's Prayer and are missing, however understandably, an opportunity to reveal the mercy of God.

❧ Evil and the God of the Parables ❧

What about the problem of Evil, says the atheist, proud of himself as he always is when he has effectively put down the believer. All right, Jesus believed in the overwhelming goodness of the Father-in-Heaven that he talked about in his parables. How can he or you explain all the tragedy of life? Couldn't that God have created a world that is better than the one we live in? A world in which there are no volcano eruptions, no earthquakes, no tsunamis, no hurricanes, no tornadoes, no floods, no famines, no heat waves, no wars, no genocide, no torture, no premature babies, no genetic freaks, no inherited disease, no sexual predators, no premature deaths of little children, no plagues, no death of anyone? Why does your God permit all those terrible tragedies?

Beats me.

Jesus who told the parables knew that his beloved Father-in-Heaven would permit him to die. How come?

I don't know.

My reply to the question of the problem of evil, a reply that is not effective to a person who doesn't want to consider an answer, is that how do you explain the problem of good? Why is there anything at all? Why does what exists fit into elaborate mathematical models? Why is there beauty? Why is there friendship? Why is there goodness? Why is there love? Why does love survive and regenerate? Why is reconciliation possible? Why do we all recognize a moral imperative, even if we do not honor it?

If the atheist then dismisses my questions with a comment that (science shows) all these phenomena are pure chance, I reply only, "Gimme a break!"

In fact, the answer to the question of whether life has meaning and purpose transcends science. It is a leap of metaphysical and/or religious faith. The pessimist sees no reason to hope but science does not constrain that conclusion and his position is not intellectually superior to that of the one who does see reason to hope. But if personality or experience or intellect incline one to the latter position then the God of the Great Parables becomes an attractive possibility. However, as John Shea puts it, that God has a lot of explaining to do.

Other Parables

W^E DO NOT know how many stories Jesus told. We have to assume, however, that most of them have been lost. Those that remain are perhaps those that were more easily remembered in the years between Jesus' return to the Father and the writing of the Gospels. Those who see conspiracies at every phase of Christian history will say that the "Church deliberately omitted the ones it found embarrassing." Yet it would be difficult to find anything more shocking than the four parables in the previous section. It seems likely that the Gospel writers themselves were ill at ease with the stories, hence the emphasis in the context of the Good Samaritan parable on a story about love of neighbors and not on the Samaritan as a metaphor for an excessive God.

Joachim Jeremias divides the parables into two categories—stories of reassurance and stories of urgency. The Good News of the kingdom in the stories in the previous section is reassuring. God loves us all and will not let us go. The stories of the farmer sowing his wheat and of the Good Shepherd offer powerful motivations for believing that God's merciful love will overcome our weakness of faith and our propensity to sin. On the other hand, the parables of urgency warn us that our time to take advantage of the mercy of the kingdom is limited. Is Jesus contradicting himself or is he changing his emphasis or does he see no contradiction between the two kinds of stories? The story of the talents does not contradict the story of the laborers at the final hour of the day. Both demand some minimal response to God's promise of mercy and love. The story of the wedding feast is not at odds with the metaphor of the mustard tree. Both guarantee that in the long run the promise of the kingdom would be achieved.

❊ *Bridesmaids and Talents* ❊

"At that time the kingdom of heaven will be like this. Once there were ten girls who took their oil lamps and went out to meet the bridegroom. Five of them were foolish, and the other five were wise. The foolish ones took their lamps with them, while the wise ones took containers full of oil for their lamps. The bridegroom was late in coming, so the girls began to nod and fall asleep.

"It was already midnight when the cry rang out, 'Here is the bridegroom! Come and meet him!' The ten girls woke up and trimmed their lamps. Then the foolish ones said to the wise ones, 'Let us have some of your oil, because our lamps are going out.' 'No,

indeed,' the wise ones answered, 'there is not enough for you and for us. Go to the store and buy some for yourselves.' So the foolish girls went off to buy some oil; and while they were gone, the bridegroom arrived. The five girls who were ready went in with him to the wedding feast, and the door was closed.

"Later the other girls arrived. 'Sir, sir! Let us in!' they cried out. 'Certainly not! I don't know you,' the bridegroom answered."

MATT. 25:1–12

Jesus did not like slackers. Would that you were hot or cold, but since you are lukewarm I will vomit you out of my mouth. The unwise bridesmaids are slackers, giddy, silly young women who wanted to be part of the dining and music and dancing at the wedding party, but as many young people of either gender do, they were not quite able to see a relation between the goal of joining the fun and the lamps that they must light for the ceremonial entrance to the marriage ceremony. The lamps were the reason they were there. If for one reason or another they could not light their lamps, then they had no claim on entering into the party. Indeed the bride had undoubtedly chosen them because she believed their beauty would impress the groom and his family. She must have assumed that they had the common sense and the responsibility to carry enough oil so that their lamps would not go out. Wait till you see my attendants, she said to the young man. There will be ten of them, five on each side, to escort you and your family into the wedding ceremony. So when the groom showed up late (in our society the opposite seems to be the more common phenomenon), he must have been startled that there were only five young women to escort his entourage. Perhaps he had made promises to his family about how elegant the circumstances of their entry was going to be. He was quite properly furious and, one must assume, so was the bride who had been let down by her friends.

The foolish and irresponsible young women behave as passive-aggressive people usually do. They blamed the wise bridesmaids. Give us some of your oil so we can go into the party. The wise bridesmaids were not about to be exploited. They were not about to be excluded from the good times. They had the good sense to understand that while it might be an embarrassment to have only five instead of the promised ten bridal attendants, it would be even worse to have none at all.

Despite the many attempts to present this story as an allegory, it is pure parable. While in the kingdom of God's love there is always forgiveness and mercy, one must always be prepared to seize the opportunities that are being offered. Those of the kingdom know that there are high stakes in life and that they must be responsible and not passive-aggressive slackers. The kingdom, which is the pearl of great price and the hidden treasure buried in the field and the widow's lost coin (in brief parables), must be pursued with energy, dedication, and passion.

The same demand for urgency is found in the parable of the talents.

❧ *Talents* ❧

So he said, "There was once a man of high rank who was going to a country far away to be made king, after which he planned to come back home. Before he left, he called his ten servants and gave them each a gold coin and told them, 'See what you can earn with this while I am gone.' Now, his countrymen hated him, and so they sent messengers after him to say, 'We don't want this man to be our king.'

"The man was made king and came back. At once he ordered his servants to appear before him, in order to find out how much they had earned. The first one came and said, 'Sir, I have earned ten gold coins with the one you gave me.' 'Well done,' he said, 'you are a good servant! Since you were faithful in small matters, I will put you in charge of ten cities.' The second servant came and said, 'Sir, I have earned five gold coins with the one you gave me.' To this one he said, 'You will be in charge of five cities.' Another servant came and said, 'Sir, here is your gold coin; I kept it hidden in a handkerchief. I was afraid of you, because you are a hard man. You take what is not yours and reap what you did not plant.' He said to him, 'You bad servant! I will use your own words to condemn you! You know that I am a hard man, taking what is not mine and reaping what I have not planted. Well then, why didn't you put my money in the bank? Then I would have received it back with interest when I

returned.' Then he said to those who were standing
there, 'Take the gold coin away from him and give it
to the servant who has ten coins.' But they said to him,
'Sir, he already has ten coins!' 'I tell you,' he replied,
'that to every person who has something, even more
will be given; but the person who has nothing, even
the little that he has will be taken away from him.' "

LUKE 19:12–26

The various puppet kings of Israel in Jewish times had to
make frequent pilgrimages to Rome to obtain and then
hold their offices. Perhaps this phenomenon was the background for the story about the king who left money with
his servants to invest while he was away. Jesus sharply con-
trasts the active and imaginative behavior of the first two
servants and the slacker, passive-aggressive response of the
third servant. I am not much good, says the third servant. I
have little ability. My master trusts me only with two talents, so he must not have much confidence in me. It's not
fair that I am just an ordinary kind of person. I'll never be
a celebrity, never be famous. I'd better play it safe. I won't
take any risks because I might lose what I have. I am a poor
and humble man. I'll show the master that it's his own
fault because he made me a poor and humble man. It is a
voice we can hear much later in history on the lips of
Charles Dickens's Uriah Heep.

Jesus liked risk takers, men and women whose open
minds and enthusiastic hearts predisposed them for the
good news of the kingdom, men like the exuberant Peter or
the publican Zacheus who was ready to make a fool out of

himself by climbing up a tree to see Jesus passing or James and John, the Sons of Thunder who wanted to call fire and brimstone down on a town that rejected them; or women like Mary of Bethany and Mary of Magdala or the Phoenician woman whose love of Jesus made them immune to the taunts of the murmurers and the begrudgers. These were Jesus' kind of people, however imperfect and incomplete their understanding or motivation might be.

The good news of the kingdom, predicted by Isaiah, demanded such responses. Jesus had a hard time with the envious, the complainers, the moaners and groaners, the slovenly, those obsessed with revenge, the lazy, the narrow, the rigid, all those who for one reason or another missed the point of his stories.

Like the scribes and the Pharisees and the temple priests.

Today such people might say I'm not as good as St. Francis or Mother Teresa or Joan of Arc, so God doesn't expect much of me. In truth, as the parable of the talents tells us, God expects everything.

❧ Stewards and Servants ❧

In a society in which the distance between the rich and the poor was so great, those who heard the stories of Jesus understood the problematic nature of relationships between master and servant. The servant was little more than a slave whose livelihood and life depended on the will—and often the whim—of the master. The unjust steward understood how the game was played, unlike the man with his pitiable two talents. However, the unmerciful servant didn't understand the game. If the master was generous to you and forgave your debt, then you must be generous to others. In both these stories we must remember that we are not hearing an allegory, but a parable with one and only one point.

Jesus said to his disciples, "There was once a rich man who had a servant who managed his property. The rich man was told that the manager was wasting his master's money, so he called him in and said, 'What is this I hear about you? Turn in a complete account of your handling of my property, because you cannot be my manager any longer.' The servant said to himself, 'My master is going to dismiss me from my job. What shall I do? I am not strong enough to dig ditches, and I am ashamed to beg. Now I know what I will do! Then when my job is gone, I shall have friends who will welcome me in their homes.' So he called in all the people who were in debt to his master. He asked the first one, 'How much do you owe my master?' 'One hundred barrels of olive oil.' The manager told him, 'Sit down and write fifty.' Then he asked another one, 'And you—how much do you owe?' 'A thousand bushels of wheat,' he answered. 'Here is your account,' the manager told him, 'write eight hundred.' As a result the master of this dishonest manager praised him for doing such a shrewd thing; because the people of this world are much more shrewd in handling their affairs than the people who belong to the light."

LUKE 16:1–18

In his advice on how those who believe in the kingdom of God's love ought to pray Jesus compares them to the woman who pesters an unjust judge so long and so vigorously that he finally gives up and grants her petition. A priest I know didn't like that image at all. There was too much corruption in the world. Jesus should not have accepted the possibility that corrupt judges should be bothered. His problem of course was that he didn't understand what a parable is about. Jesus was hardly praising the judge. It is strange how people can pull something out of context and miss the whole point. One can argue that it is all Jesus' fault for telling such troubling stories.

In the parable of the unjust steward, however, he seems to have pushed the envelope even further. The cheating steward is the hero of the story. He is praised for his cleverness. He is not able to dig and he is ashamed to beg. Therefore he indulges in something like graft. Most likely he had been cheating his master all along, taking a coin here and a coin there and making a few modifications in the accounting. He was a loser but a very clever loser. Apparently he had no reason to fear for his life because he did not try to cover his tracks. The master found out and praised him for his ingenuity, an odd reaction to such blatant dishonesty.

That story must have shocked those who heard it. What in the world did Jesus mean by it? St. Luke provides a helpful interpretation, which might not be based on anything Jesus said since Jesus did not like to explain his parables (no storyteller likes to be asked for explanations). However the irony does sound like Jesus. The story, however, adds to the demands for an appropriate response to the good news. One must not only be enthusiastic, one must be clever, ingenious, maybe just a little tricky. One must seek ways to pass on the good news to others that are attractive to those to whom one wants to preach the Gospel, a requirement not always honored by those who aim to preach it—perhaps because it often seems more efficient to scare people than to win them. Perhaps one must create great art, beautiful churches, sublime music, beautiful poetry, compelling stories.

Perhaps also one must forgive.

"Because the kingdom of heaven is like this. Once there was a king who decided to check on his servants' accounts. He had just begun to do so when one of them was brought in who owed him millions of dollars. The servant did not have enough to pay his debt, so the king ordered him to be sold as a slave, with his wife and his children and all that he had, in order to pay the debt. The servant fell on his knees before the king. 'Be patient with me,' he begged, 'and I will pay you everything!' The king felt sorry for him, so he forgave him the debt and let him go.

"Then the man went out and met one of his fellow servants who owed him a few dollars. He grabbed him and started choking him. 'Pay back what you owe me!' he said. His fellow servant fell down and begged him, 'Be patient with me, and I will pay you back!' But he refused; instead, he had him thrown into jail until he should pay the debt. When the other servants saw what had happened, they were very upset and went to the king and told him everything. So he called the

servant in. 'You worthless slave!' he said. 'I forgave you the whole amount you owed me just because you asked me to. You should have had mercy on your fellow servant, just as I had mercy on you.' The king was very angry, and he sent the servant to jail to be punished until he should pay back the whole amount."

MATT. 18:23–34

The story of the forgiven one who will not forgive, told in response to Peter's suggestion that forgiving his brother seven times is enough, is one of the most blunt and most harrowing stories in the New Testament. We flee from its brutal lesson because it is so unpalatable. We cannot negotiate with God that he forgive us. That has already happened. Our contrition, our promises of amendment, our vows to reform our life, do not earn that which is freely given. But heaven help us (quite literally) if we are not willing to extend forgiveness to others. The plea for forgiveness in the Lord's Prayer is a promise—as you forgive us, so we forgive others. There is no room for hatred, cruelty, revenge in the kingdom of the Father-in-Heaven.

Those who have lost someone they love to a predatory human monster have no license to spit out their hatred for the monster in a courtroom display that mocks the teachings of Jesus and the mercy and love of the Father-in-Heaven. Does this mean we must forgive the World Trade Center bombers? Or the Japanese who raped Nanking in China? Or the Germans responsible for the Holocaust? Or Hitler? Or Stalin?

The answer from within the kingdom must be a resounding "Yes!"

"Don't even ask."

Or "What is it about 'judge not that you be not judged' that you don't understand?"

We must defend our rights and the rights of those we love. We may not be able to blot out the memories of injustices, large and small, that have been worked on us. However we should not treasure in our imaginations fantasies of "getting even" with these enemies. I personally must resist the ever powerful temptation to respond in kind to hate mail. When possible we should seek reconciliation. In the kingdom of God's mercy and love there is no room for hatred, none at all.

This is a hard saying, but Jesus said it in one way or another many times over. Somehow or the other, many of those who profess to be followers of Jesus don't seem to have heard it. They are not at all embarrassed when they violate his command that we forgive our fellow servants who perhaps do not know what they do.

So the kingdom of the Father-in-Heaven requires of its citizens that they be dedicated, enthusiastic, relentless, and forgiving. Just like Jesus. It may be an attractive place (though filled with a lot of foreigners), but the cost of admission is high.

✸ Banquets and Vineyards ✸

The gift of the kingdom can be lost. One can ignore it because of indifference or turn against it in anger. Neither behavior is uncommon. Whether the people who deliberately reject the kingdom of God's mercy and love will nonetheless be pursued by God's relentless compassion so that they finally accept his last and best offer is an open question. God's mercy, as theologian Karl Rahner suggested, is stronger than his justice. Nonetheless Jesus found it necessary in some of his stories to appeal to fear of the Lord, admittedly only the beginning of wisdom, but in some cases a good beginning.

Jesus said to him, "There was once a man who was giving a great feast to which he invited many people. When it was time for the feast, he sent his servant to tell his guests, 'Come, everything is ready!' But they all began, one after another, to make excuses. The first one told the servant, 'I have bought a field and must go and look at it; please accept my apologies.' Another one said, 'I have bought five pairs of oxen and am on my way to try them out; please accept my apologies.' Another one said, 'I have just gotten married, and for that reason I cannot come.' The servant went back and told all this to his master. The master was furious and said to his servant, 'Hurry out to the streets and alleys of the town, and bring back the poor, the crippled, the blind, and the lame.' Soon the servant said, 'Your order has been carried out, sir, but there is room for no more.' So the master said to the servant, 'Go out to the country roads and lanes and make people come in, so that my house will be full. I tell you all that none of those men who were invited will taste my dinner!' "

LUKE 14:16–24

Only a fool turns down an invitation to a great feast with such weak excuses as proffered in this story. Bring your wife along. Surely your oxen and field can wait till the feast is over. The feast-giver had every right to feel insulted. The excusers' replies were contemptuous. In those days, perhaps, there were no such people as the "no-shows"—people who accept the invitation but find an excuse at the very last minute and don't come to the banquet table.

One must insist that this story is a parable, not an allegory. Hence it has only one point—the host does not need them, he can "paper the house" by going to the highways and the byways and bring in guests who would be only too happy to eat the good food, drink the excellent wine, and listen to the lovely music. The host was not demanding that the invited guests do him a favor by coming to his party. The invitation to enter the kingdom is not to a command performance. It is rather an invitation to a joyous experience. If you're too busy with other things or are, for some reason, angry at God, that's up to you. Don't think you'll spoil God's day by blowing him off.

To equate the rude invitees with the Jewish people, as perhaps the early Christians did (even perhaps St. Luke), is to allegorize the parable and deprive it of its punch. No religious or ethnic group has a monopoly on this kind of infidelity. Indifference is part of the human condition. We drift along in our busy lives, distracted by our many obligations, enchanted by our many toys, worried about our many problems. Jesus is an attractive figure, the promises of the kingdom are appealing. If only we had more time. Next year, I will take God more seriously. Or after the kids get back to school. Or after the holidays. Or after I have the house cleaned properly. Or after I try this case or complete this deal. Or after the children are in college and the dog is dead.

And thus does time run out.

> *Then Jesus told the people this parable: "There was once a man who planted a vineyard, rented it out to tenants, and then left home for a long time. When the time came to gather the grapes, he sent a slave to the tenants to receive from them his share of the harvest. But the tenants beat the slave and sent him back without a thing. So he sent another slave; but the tenants beat him also, treated him shamefully, and sent him back without a thing. Then he sent a third slave; the tenants wounded him, too, and threw him out. Then the owner of the vineyard said, 'What shall I do? I will send my own dear son; surely they will respect him!' But when the tenants saw him, they said to one another, 'This is the owner's son. Let's kill him, and his property will be ours!' So they threw him out of the vineyard and killed him.*
>
> *"What, then, will the owner of the vineyard do to the tenants?" Jesus asked. "He will come and kill those men, and turn the vineyard over to other tenants."*
>
> *When the people heard this, they said, "Surely not!"*
>
> LUKE 20:9–16

The story of the vineyard (a favorite metaphor in both the Jewish and Christian Scriptures) is perhaps the harshest of all Jesus' parables. Again one must resist the temptation to allegorize it and free our own consciences by blaming the Jewish people. Jesus is rather talking about the enemies of the kingdom, those who want to take it over and use it for themselves—for their own wealth and power. The good news is left in charge of religious leaders and in some times and places political leaders who have intruded themselves into the religious game.

Who are the enemies within the kingdom itself who wish to use it for their own purposes? Politicians who use religion to support their own agenda, priests who run their parish as if it is a medieval fief, lay staff members who use their position to convert parishioners to their personal ideology, bishops who covered up the pedophile crisis to protect their power, bishops who use the Eucharist as a tool to control Catholic politicians and thus try to recoup their power, curial bureaucrats who treat the rest of the Church as their own plaything, theologians who pontificate about Catholic people who in fact know nothing about them, ultraconservatives who write nasty letters complaining about their priests, some of the so-called John Paul II priests who profess that the laity must learn to obey them. And on and on.

Readers who are not Catholic can list their own members who think they own the church.

This is a different take on the story of the vineyard than those you will hear in weekend homilies. Yet it seems consistent with the story of those who have been given a temporary lease on power in the Church and then act as if they own it.

No one owns the kingdom, no one except God. Those who think they own it or act like they own it are idolaters. They are perverting the fire that created the cosmos.

The first four parables describe for us the shape of the kingdom of God's mercy and love. The second group of stories—bridesmaids and talents, stewards and servants, banquets and vineyards—tell us how we should respond to the opportunity inherent in the kingdom of mercy and love. We should be ingenious and dedicated enthusiasts, utterly committed to revealing the forgiveness that is the essence of the kingdom and to respecting the kingdom with holy awe, less we profane it by our idolatry.

❈ Jesus' Parable About Himself ❈

Jesus often referred to himself as the "Son of Man," an allusion (perhaps) to a messianic figure in the book of Daniel. However, the favorite image of early Christian artists and, one suspects, of Jesus himself, is that of the good shepherd. The author of St. John's Gospel apparently had several such comparisons available among his resources when he wrote the tenth chapter of his story. He combined them in one discourse, regardless of the fact that the meaning of the metaphor changes as he leapt from image to image.

> *"I am the good shepherd, who is willing to die for the sheep. When the hired man, who is not a shepherd and does not own the sheep, sees a wolf coming, he leaves*

the sheep and runs away; so the wolf snatches the sheep and scatters them. The hired man runs away because he is only a hired man and does not care about the sheep. I am the good shepherd. As the Father knows me and I know the Father, in the same way I know my sheep and they know me. There are other sheep which belong to me that are not in this sheep pen. I must bring them, too; they will listen to my voice, and they will become one flock with one shepherd."

JOHN 10:11-16

The earliest known Christian art depicted a young man with a lamb over his shoulder, an extension of St. John's litany of images to include the parable of the shepherd who (like the woman with the lost coin) leaves the ninety-nine sheep behind and seeks the one that is lost. Like all good metaphors, the parable of the good shepherd ("I am the good shepherd") is dense and polysemous—it admits of many complementary interpretations. Jesus is the gate of the sheepfold, the protector of the sheep against those who would harm them, the one who gives them a more abundant life. He knows his sheep and they know him. He will lay down his life for his sheep. He has other sheep that he must gather into the sheepfold so that there will be one flock and one shepherd. The central metaphor is that of a shepherd who has an intimate and affectionate relationship with each of his sheep.

The image exists also in the Jewish Scriptures. In Psalm 22(23) the poet says confidently that the Holy One is his shepherd who protects him in verdant pastures. Yet the comparison is surprising. Shepherds were dirty, smelly, uncouth men, ignorant of the niceties of civilized life and of the requirements of the Torah. They were at the bottom of the social class scale, the lowliest of the low, regarded with the same disdain that many today would have for "hillbillies" or "rednecks" or "illegals." Yet they were invited by angels to the manger scene at Bethlehem and Jesus identified with them. Moreover sheep are, as everyone in his time knew from experience, dumb, pathetic, foolish creatures. It was not a compliment to define people as sheep, perhaps on their way to the slaughter. The parable of the good shepherd is therefore transgressive. It is not one that the Gospel writers would have dared to make up themselves. We have become so used to it that we don't realize how it might seem to degrade both Jesus and us.

Why then is the image of the good shepherd so powerful down through Christian history? Why do artists love it so much? Perhaps because the members of the flock are so utterly dependent on the loving care of the shepherd and because the shepherd's affection for his defenseless sheep is so gentle and tender. From the point of view of Jesus (and the Father-in-Heaven for whom he is himself a metaphor) we may be weak, stupid, and fragile creatures, silly, confused, and easily frightened. Just the same he loves us and takes care of us. Therefore everything will be all right, all will be well as Lady Juliana said, all will be well and all manner of things will be well.

The good shepherd parable therefore is nothing more than a continuation of the parable of the Good Samaritan. God is excessive in his mercy and love.

If one reads the Gospels searching for the stories and the metaphors—mindful that the authors say that Jesus taught through stories—one encounters an exciting and disturbing picture of Jesus and of the kingdom of the Father-in-Heaven.

In these stories we encounter the real Jesus. Most of the Jesus Seminar critics, including Robert Funk, agree that the stories are so outrageous that no one in the early Church would dare to have made them up. The rest of the Gospel accounts are important, of course, but if you want to know what Jesus was really like and what he really believed, if you want to get to the "essential" Jesus, then you must read and reread the parables.

One must suspend the interpretations one has heard in school and church, the dull and uninteresting guise in which we normally encounter the stories of Jesus, and open oneself to surprise and wonder. Why does Jesus compare himself to the most repulsive and rejected members of the working class? Why does he compare the Father-in-Heaven to a compulsive and excessive Samaritan, an irresponsible judge who dismisses a charge of adultery without hearing the evidence, a foolish vineyard owner who pays a day's wage to those who have worked less than an hour? An indulgent father who spoils his two worthless sons rotten?

If we are able to ask those questions, then we begin to understand why the crowds followed after Jesus and why he became a threat to the political and religious powers of his day, why he had to die.

The Final Story

A FTER HIS INTENSE experience of the Father-in-Heaven on Mount Tabor, Jesus, as the Gospels say, set his face toward Jerusalem because it was necessary that a prophet die in Jerusalem. Why, we must ask, the rush? Why cut short his ministry after a couple of years? Would it not have been better to live for many more years, to tell many more stories, to gather more followers around him, to train his rather dubious core of leaders, to leave a more detailed historical record?

In the Transfiguration experience, Jesus understood that it was necessary to die for the kingdom and that the Father-in-Heaven would vindicate him. He was probably aware that his enemies—the suspicious Romans, the frightened temple priesthood, and the Pharisees—were closing in on him. He was too popular. He was a threat, a danger, an infection that must be eradicated. His time was up. He had done his best to preach the vision of Isaiah and to tell the crowds about the Father-in-Heaven. Now all that was left was to die. He had run the course, as St. Paul would later say.

When they arrived in Jerusalem, Jesus went to the Temple and began to drive out all those who were buying and selling. He overturned the tables of the money-changers and the stools of those who sold pigeons, and he would not let anyone carry anything through the temple courtyards. He then taught the people. "It is written in the Scriptures that God said, 'My Temple will be called a house of prayer for the people of all nations.' But you have turned it into a hideout for thieves!"

The chief priests and the teachers of the Law heard of this, so they began looking for some way to kill Jesus. They were afraid of him, because the whole crowd was amazed at his teaching.

When evening came, Jesus and his disciples left the city.

MARK 11:15–19

Since he was human Jesus had to die. Moreover he had to die with such faith in his vindication by the Father-in-Heaven that he would show all his followers how to die. Down through the ages, whenever one of us dies, Jesus would be there to go down into the valley of death with us, to console us and to promise us that death would not have the final victory over us.

Under the circumstances that existed at that time, he did nothing to placate his enemies. His assault on the temple asked for trouble. Yet why did he do it? The incident is described by John in the early chapters of his Gospel, but Matthew and Mark stage it in the last week of his life. The latter choice seems more probable both because the cleansing of the temple is a statement, indeed an act of defiance from a man who knew he was about to die and because it is not likely that he would have begun his public life by picking a fight with the temple priesthood.

But why take them on? Was he not defying the law of the Torah? Who did he think he was? my friend Jacob Neusner asks in his illuminating dialogue with Rabbi Jesus. While the assault on the temple does not bother most Christians, it deeply offends many Jews because they think he is rejecting the Jewish heritage.

The answer to Rabbi Neusner, I think, is that he thought he was the direct representative of the Father-in-Heaven, missioned to preach again the vision of Isaiah to Israel. He saw the temple customs and priesthood as incompatible with that vision, especially since women and gentiles were excluded from the main religious areas of the temple. He also deplored the payments that were being extorted, as he saw it, from the devout. The temple priesthood was an affluent elite using religion for their own personal profit.

Criticism of the temple religion—not as it should have been in theory but as it was in practice—was widespread at that time. Jesus was not the only critic. The Pharisees, who were not allied to the temple priests, were equally critical. Jesus cleansed the temple, not because he rejected the Jewish heritage, but because he firmly believed it, especially as it was seen by Isaiah and Daniel. As I noted at the beginning of this essay, attempts to depict Jesus as an apostate are anachronistic because they judge him by the more rigorous stands of rabbinic Judaism that came into being much later. The symbolic cleansing of the temple (and it may not have been a major intrusion) was a protest from the viewpoint of a Galilean Jew who took Isaiah and Daniel very seriously.

It also contributed to the agitation for his death.

I will not discuss the details of that death. Those who were overwhelmed by the suffering of Jesus in *The Passion of the Christ* lament the terrible things they did to him. They don't seem to understand that in those days crucifixion was commonplace, Rome's brutal but routine form of capital punishment and something that Jews must have witnessed often. Jesus was born in a cave, lived as an impoverished peasant, and died as a falsely charged criminal—none of which marked him as different from hundreds of thousands of others. Rome crucified six thousand prisoners from the Spartacus revolution (not including Spartacus himself who, contrary to the film, was already dead) along the Appian Way between Rome and Capua.

That it was a frequent occurrence does not make crucifixion any less horrible or the sufferings of Jesus any less intense. It means rather that it was not extraordinary. The fans of Mel Gibson respond by saying, "Yes, but consider whom they were killing!" Indeed yes, but consider also that Jesus chose a criminal's execution to make common cause with all the innocent victims of cruel executions through the many centuries of human existence up to and including the deaths of brother Jews in the Holocaust, the mass murders in Cambodia and Rwanda, and the killings of the innocent in Darfur and Iraq at the time of this writing. And the victims of the judicial murders England committed in Ireland for half a millennium. *The Passion of the Christ* did not seem to understand that unity between Jesus and all innocent victims and indeed between Jesus and all humankind. Nor did it have anything to say about the stories Jesus told that so infuriated his enemies that they wanted to kill him. Finally, the film does not report the evidence that the Father-in-Heaven vindicated Jesus a couple of days later—not even the charming encounter on the road to Emmaus that I quoted at the beginning of the book. A voyeuristic obsession caused the filmmaker to miss the point. And the greatest story of all.

And the wildest surprise of all.

Conclusion

❧

THE FINAL ISSUE about the stories of Jesus (and the stories told about him) is whether they are true. I do not mean whether Jesus was fabricating the stories. Clearly he was not. He did believe that the Father-in-Heaven was like the Good Samaritan, the Indulgent Father, the Lenient Judge, the Crazy Vintner. He also believed that the kingdom, foreseen by Isaiah, that the Father sent him to announce was a treasure buried in a field and a pearl of great price. He believed that it was a kingdom of dedication and forgiveness, a great gift to accept while there was still time, and a gift to be protected from both indifference and perversion by those who would use it to promote their own wealth and power. He also believed that he was indeed the good shepherd. He was a man of surprises, a surprise himself (especially in his treatment of women), and he preached the good news of a Great Surprise.

There can be no doubt that a careful reading of the stories of Jesus, a reading free of the influence of bad homilies and poor spirituality, supports this view of Jesus. He was neither a prevaricator nor an apostate as some of his enemies have claimed. But was he a victim of self-deception? Had he been hypnotized by the dazzling mysticism of Isaiah and Daniel? Was he a gifted storyteller, a man of immense presence and charm, a magnetic leader who in the final analysis deceived himself by the haunting mystery of his stories?

Does the Father-in-Heaven really exist?

If he does, then no other being is worthy of the name God. No more attractive and compelling portrait of God has ever been created. The Father-in-Heaven is the only God worth believing in. Is this Person who is nothing more than mercy and love really the animating power of the universe, the one who created the Big Bang with us (and perhaps many more) in mind?

The answer to that question depends on a leap of faith, not a blind leap surely, but a reasoned leap into wonder and mystery and surprise.